Jade

木碢圖說

鋼碢磨畢玉體雖平淨然尚欠光亮即用木碢及浸水黃寶料或用各色沙漿以磨之

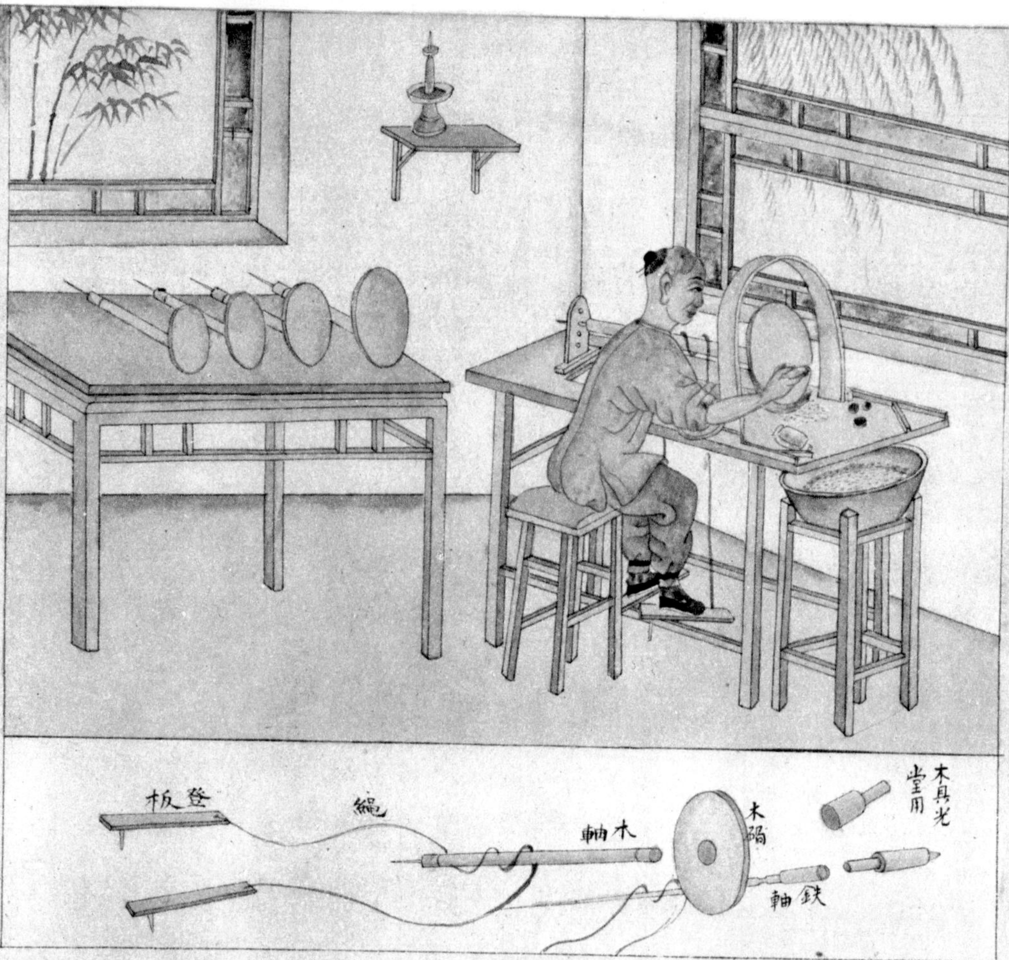

若小件玉器不能用木碢磨之或有甚細窰花樣者皆不可用木碢磨之則以乾葫蘆片作小碢以磨之

十三皮碢圖說

此係皮碢磨亮上光之圖也碢係牛皮為之包于木碢之上納以麻繩大者尺餘見圖小則二三寸不等皆用沁水寶

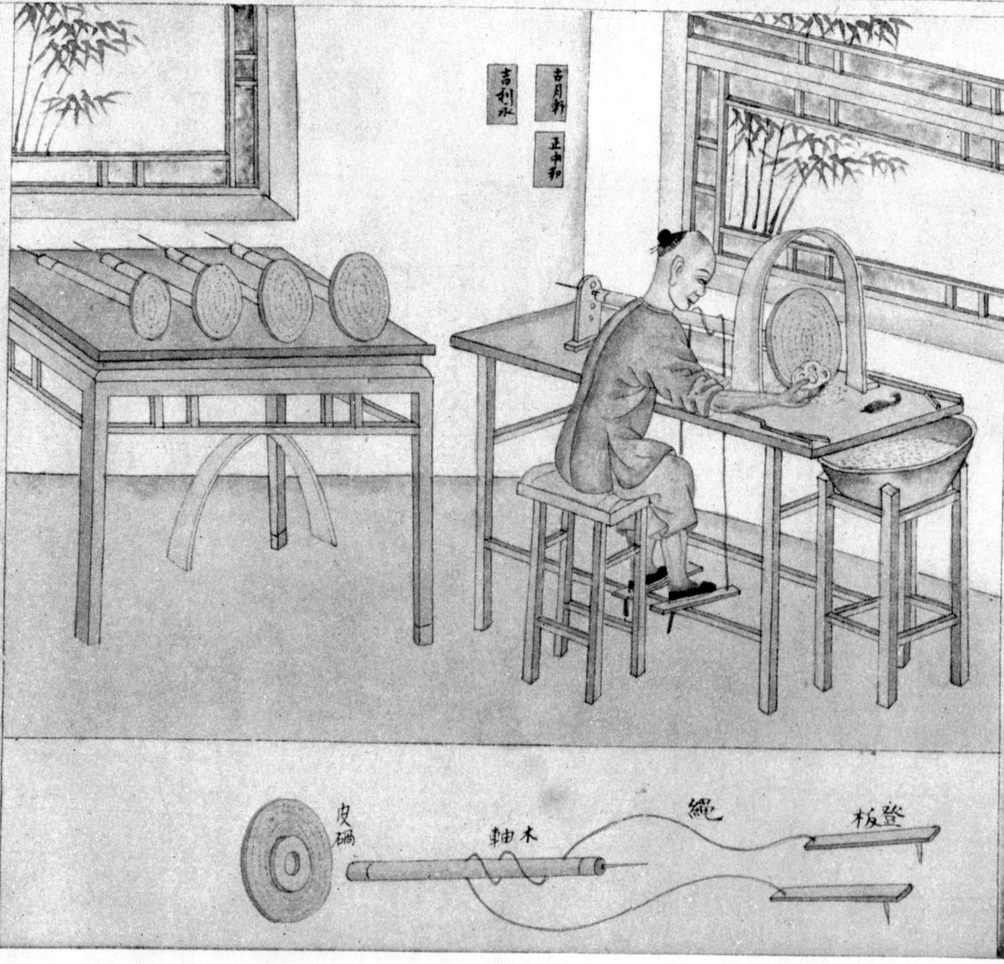

料磨之皮碢上光後則玉體光亮溫潤使鑒家愛之無窮至此則琢磨工事畢矣

SPRING ART BOOKS

Jade

BY J. P. PALMER

SPRING BOOKS · LONDON

ACKNOWLEDGMENTS

The pieces in this volume are reproduced by kind permission of the following collections and galleries to which they belong: Sir Alan Barlow Bt, G.C.B. Buckinghamshire (plates 12, 17); British Museum, London (plates 2, 3, 4, 6, 7, 16, 26, 39, 42, 44, 50, 51, 52, 53); Dumbarton Oaks, Washington D.C., Robert Woods Bliss Collection of Pre-Columbian Art (plates 49, 54); Fitzwilliam Museum, Cambridge (plates 1, 5, 10, 13, 18, 19, 20, 23, 33, 35, 36); Fundação Calouste Gulbenkian, Oeiras, Portugal (plate 38); Mrs Howard Hansford, Surrey (plate 37); Krolik Collection, London (plates 29, 30, 31); George de Menasce O.B.E., London (plates 27, 28, 34); Nelson Gallery—Atkins Museum, Nelson Fund, Kansas City (plate 8); University Museum of Archeology and Ethnology, Cambridge (plates 46, 47, 48); Victoria and Albert Museum, London (plates 9, 11, 14, 15, 25, 40, 41, 43, 45); Sir Isaac Wolfson Bt, London (plates 24, 32). The black and white photographs in this volume are reproduced by kind permission of: British Museum, London (figures 4, 6, 8); The Mount Trust, Churchill, Oxfordshire (figure 2); Victoria and Albert Museum, London (figure 5); Walker Art Center, Minneapolis (figure 7); The frontispiece and figure 3 are reproduced from *Investigations and Studies in Jade. The Heber R, Bishop Collection.* Vol. I, New York. Privately printed 1906.

The following photographs were supplied by Michael Holford, London: Plates 1, 2, 3, 4, 5, 6, 7, 9, 10, 11, 12, 13, 14, 15, 16, 17, 18, 19, 20, 21, 22, 23, 24, 25, 26, 27, 28, 29, 30, 31, 32, 33, 34, 35, 36, 37, 39, 40, 41, 42, 43, 44, 45, 46, 47, 48, 50, 51, 52, 53, figures 4, 5, 6.

Published by
SPRING BOOKS
Drury House · Russell Street · London WC2
© Paul Hamlyn Ltd 1967
Printed in Czechoslovakia by Polygrafia, Prague
T 1734

CONTENTS

THE BLACK AND WHITE ILLUSTRATIONS

INTRODUCTION

To the minds of many people, the word jade suggests three things — the colour green, the land of China, and a piece of jewellery. These scraps of information are only a minute fraction of a story that involves not only China but also America, Persia, India and New Zealand and covers a period in time of some 4,000 years, and the colours of this precious stone range from green to blue, to yellow and red, white and black — in a wide variety of shades. The story of jade also involves an account of a highly specialised branch of the stone carver's art, for the skill required to carve a piece of this most intractable stone is considerable.

A piece of carved jade can be compared in some ways to a cut diamond. Both are valued for their rarity and the skill required in their cutting, and for the beauty of their colour and both are extremely hard. But whereas the diamond flashes and sparkles in the light, a piece of jade, because of its translucence, catches the light and reflects it back with an even quality that might almost be said to be glowing. The cold hard smooth feel of a piece of jade provides a sense of pleasure that can never be obtained from a diamond — a special quality observed by the Chinese and included by them as one of its greatest virtues.

In China, jade has always been valued more highly than any other precious stone. Apart from its physical qualities (compared by the Confucians with the qualities necessary for a virtuous life) it was endowed with a mystical religious significance that has no parallel among precious stones in the western world. Because of its rarity, the Aztecs offered jade as gifts to the conquering Spaniards — who were somewhat surprised, and the Maoris of New Zealand were prepared to face great danger in order to obtain it.

No mention is made of jade in European literature until the early Spanish navigators returned with specimens of green stones collected from the natives of Central and South America. The Spaniards claimed that these stones would cure diseases of the kidneys and gave them the name *piedra de hijada*, meaning 'stone of the loins' or 'colic stone'. This allegedly therapeutic effect gave rise to the name nephrite, from *nephros*, the Greek word for the kidneys. In French the word became *l'ejade* and during the seventeenth century, by a process of error, this was transformed into the masculine word *le jade*. This stone was first brought to England at the end of the sixteenth century by Sir Walter Raleigh who always referred to it by its Spanish name of *hijada*. The word *jade* first occurs in England in 1727 in *Chambers' Cyclopedia*.

Considerable confusion as to the exact nature of jade existed until the middle of the nineteenth century. Other stones, including jasper, were often included under this term. Sir Hans Sloane (1660-1753), the natural historian and founder of the British Museum, writing about the natural history of Jamaica in the early eighteenth century, called *piedra de hijada* 'green jasper'. In 1863 Alexis Damour, an eminent French chemist, established the fact that jade was really two minerals. He worked on a number of pieces of jade carving brought to France from China, as part of the loot obtained when the Summer Palace, near Peking, was destroyed in 1860 by Anglo-French forces as a reprisal for the ill-treatment of Europeans during the T'ai P'ing rebellion of 1859-60. For one of these he retained the name *jade* or *nephrite*. The other mineral was given the name *jadeite* some time later, in 1881. Although these investigations had established the true nature of jade, the choice of names has been the source of considerable confusion. The mineral he chose to call nephrite was not in fact the stone imported into Europe by the Spaniards as this had all been jadeite. The two names have however been retained and the word *jade* is used generally unless it is necessary to make some distinction between the two minerals.

THE PHYSICAL PROPERTIES OF JADEITE AND NEPHRITE

Jadeite and nephrite do possess certain similarities in their physical properties (notably their hardness), but differ in their chemical composition and crystalline structure. Nephrite is a calcium-magnesium silicate belonging to the amphibole group of minerals. Its crystalline structure is built up of long fibrous crystals closely matted together. It has a specific gravity of about 3.0 — varying from 2.9 to 3.1.

Jadeite is a sodium aluminium silicate, with a crystalline structure made up of groups of small granular crystals. It belongs to the pyroxene group of minerals. This stone has a constant specific gravity of 3.33. Both these stones are translucent, nephrite usually rather more so than jadeite.

Both nephrite and jadeite are extremely hard. A scale for assessing the relative hardness of various naturally occurring substances was devised by the Austrian mineralogist

Friedrich Mohs in 1820. The softest material on the Mohs Scale is talc, and this is given a value of 1; the hardest is the diamond, which is placed at 10. On this scale, nephrite is placed at $6^1/_2$ and jadeite at $6^3/_4$. Although their hardness does differ, it is too slight to be used for distinguishing between them. Since ordinary steel ranks at not more than $6^1/_2$ on the Mohs Scale, the surface of jade will not be scratched by the blade of a pocket knife, and this test may be applied to discover whether or not a stone is jade. Care should be taken to apply this test only to surfaces that have not undergone any chemical change caused by burial or by burning, for areas affected in this way are softer and scratch easily. The scratch test will not work on certain minerals of the serpentine group, which may be confused with jade. This applies particularly to bowenite which has a hardness of 6. This stone has been carved by the Maoris of New Zealand and closely resembles jade.

If this scratch test does not prove to be successful for determining whether a stone is jade, more elaborate tests must be carried out. These involve the determination of the specific gravity of the mineral, the measurement of its refractive index or X-ray crystal analysis. These tests can also be used for differentiating beween nephrite and jadeite. The specific gravity test is of no use when the jade has been decomposed in either of the ways mentioned above.

It is possible in some instances to distinguish by their appearance nephrite and jadeite that have been carved and polished. The surface of nephrite takes on a much less glossy finish than that of jadeite. Certain differences also occur in their colour.

The colour of jade is caused by the presence of small quantities of various chemicals, mainly compounds of iron, manganese, and chromium. Pure jade is white, but according to the type and the amount of the impurity the colours range through various shades of green, blue, brown, yellow and grey, to black. The commonest colour is green, and the dark green colour of nephrite is caused by the presence of iron in the form of ferrous silicate. The apple-green and emerald-green colours that are characteristic of jadeite are produced by chromium. The widespread use of green jadeite in modern China, for making jewellery for export to America and Europe, has given rise to the use of the word jade-green. The much sought after 'mutton fat' jade — which is white and has the appearance of congealed fat — is nephrite. Mauve and light blue are colours only found in jadeite. A form of jadeite which is black in colour, due to the presence of a high concentration of an iron compound, is called chloromelanite.

The appearance of nephrite may be altered by artificial means, such as burial over a long period of time, or by burning in a fire. All the jades dating from the Han dynasty (206 B.C. — A.D. 220) and before, illustrated in this book, show signs of having been buried. Nephrite, when subjected to high temperatures changes to an opaque substance resembling bone, without the shape of the object altering in any way. The Chinese call this 'chicken bone' white. Both burial and burning reduce the hardness of the nephrite. Jadeite is not affected by heat until the temperature reaches 1025 °C., when it liquefies to a colourless glass.

Pebbles and boulders of jade that have been weathered over a long period of time develop an outer 'skin' which is usually brown in colour, but some jadeite pebbles have a tomato red 'skin'. This skin may be cut away before the jade carver starts his work, or it may be used as part of the decorative scheme.

WHERE JADE IS FOUND

Discoveries of naturally occurring jade have been reported from many areas in the world. In Europe, Asia, North and South America and parts of Polynesia it was used in prehistoric times for making simple implements. Heinrich Fischer of Freiburg, in the middle of the nineteenth century, put forward the theory that all jade was obtained from Asia, including that of Europe and South America. In Europe this theory was proved to be wrong by the discovery of jade in situ at Jordansmühl, in Poland, in 1884, and later at a number of other places.

In 1954 jadeite was discovered in Guatemala, thus providing a provenance for the material used by the Mayas and other pre-Columbian civilisations of Central America. Jadeite has also been found in California, and nephrite in Alaska, Wyoming and in Brazil.

In the Pacific area, the largest supply of nephrite comes from a small area on the west coast of the South Island of New Zealand, situated between two river valleys — those of the Taramakau and the Arehura. The mouths of these two rivers are about nine miles apart. The stone was collected from the river beds and on beaches where pebbles and small boulders that had been carried out to sea were thrown back on to the land. These stones on the seashore gave rise to the legend that they were originally fish which had been caught and brought on to the beach, where they were fastened and eventually changed into jade. This is probably the region that is referred to by the Maoris as *Wai-pounamu*, or 'Water of Pounamu'.

The range of the southern Alps inland, and the dangerous coastline, made this area particularly difficult to approach. Being the only area where the Maoris could obtain jade, the natives of the North Island thought of the South Island as the land of jade.

Jade has also been discovered in the Griffin Range and near Lake Wakatipu, both areas on the South Island. Jade, mainly nephrite, has been reported from New Caledonia, the New Hebrides, New Guinea and Tasmania. The first discovery of jade in Africa was made in 1960 in Southern Rhodesia.

The most important source of nephrite in Asia is the area round Khotan and Yarkand in Chinese Turkestan. At least since Han times (206 B.C. — A.D. 220) China's main supply of nephrite — 'true jade' — has come from this area. During the periods in history when imperial expansion was at its greatest, this area sent tribute to the emperor — part of this tribute being jade.

Both these towns are situated at the foot of the K'un Lun Mountains, a range which rises on the border of China proper and forms the boundary between Chinese Turkestan and Tibet. The oasis of Khotan is near the meeting point of two rivers — the Karakash or Black Jade River, and the Yurung-kash or White Jade River. Both these rivers have their source in the K'un Lun Mountains. Yarkand is some distance to the north west of Khotan. Marco Polo, on his way to China in 1472 visited Khotan, and mentions stones — which he calls jasper and chalcedony, but which were in fact jade — that were collected in this area and exported to China.

Pebbles and boulders of jade were found in river beds, or the stone was quarried in the mountains. In the quarries, fires were lit near the veins of jade and when the heat had cracked the stone, wedges were driven into the cracks and large pieces of jade were broken away.

Nephrite has also been imported into China from the region round Lake Baikal in Siberia. A highly prized variety of nephrite that is green with black specks of graphite embedded in the stone, called 'spinach jade' by the Chinese, has been found only in this area. During the late nineteenth and early twentieth centuries, nephrite from Siberia was used in Russia for making jewellery and other small objects, notably by Carl Fabergé. Although no tradition of jade carving was ever established in Europe, gem cutters in the sixteenth century produced a number of objects in this material. Three pieces of dark green jade — two covered bowls each standing on a high foot, and a covered urn — all distinctly European in design, are to be found among the French crown jewels, now on exhibition in the Louvre. All these pieces are very much in the style of sixteenth century Italian rock crystal carving. A large block of Siberian nephrite was used for the sarcophagus of Czar Alexander III (1845 — 1894).

Jadeite was mined in much the same way in the area of the Chindwin and Uru rivers in north Burma. Operations can only be carried on in this region from March to May during the rainy season when other work has to stop. The mines at this time are flooded and have to be emptied by pumping. In recent times, modern methods and equipment have been introduced including the use of dynamite and pneumatic drills.

Small quantities of jade in situ have been reported from a number of other Asian countries including India and Japan. Although a number of finds have been reported, it has not yet been definitely established that jade occurs within the boundary of the equipment eighteen provinces of China.

CHINA

Of all the countries where Neolithic people made simple implements of jade, China is the only one where the technique of carving was developed in later periods and is still being carried on today.

The character used by the Chinese for jade is *yü*. The earliest version of *yü* appears on oracle inscriptions of the Shang dynasty. These records were carved on bones and tortoiseshell and were used in connection with the interpretation of oracles. In a glossary of the second or third century B.C. which gives the explanation of terms used in ancient writings, *yü* does not appear under a separate heading, but this character is found among the definitions of other terms. From these it would appear to mean a valuable stone used for making ceremonial paraphernalia. During the second century A.D. a dictionary, called the *Shuo wen* was compiled, and in this *yü* is defined from three different points of view.

'*Yü* — a stone that is beautiful.

It has five virtues, there is warmth in its lustre and brilliancy, this is the manner of kindness;

its interior may be viewed from outside, revealing (the goodness) within, this is the manner of rectitude;

its note is tranquil and high and carries far and wide, this is the way of wisdom and it may be broken but cannot be twisted, this is the manner of bravery; its sharp edges are not intended for violence, this is the way of purity.

The second definition incorporates the virtues of jade that had been enumerated in earlier works such as the *Li-chi* which is attributed to Confucius and embodies the moral feeling of his teachings. The qualities of lustre and translucency, its use for making musical stones, its toughness and its ability to take and keep a sharp edge are certainly things which commended jade to Chinese connoisseurs in all later periods. Because of its long associations with these virtues, the character for jade came to be used

The Chinese character for yü *is shown above in its archaic and present day forms.*

as an adjective, expressing the qualities of beauty, nobility and purity.

It can be seen from the first of these definitions that *yü* can be applied to any stone that is beautiful. This has caused some difficulty and confusion when interpreting or translating texts where this character is used. It is perhaps fitting that *yü* should be translated into 'jade'; a word meaning more than one material. To distinguish jade from the other 'beautiful' stones, the Chinese use the expression *Chen yü*.

In China, true jade means nephrite. Jadeite, which was introduced into China from northern Burma through the province of Yunnan is called *Yunnan yü* or *fei-ts'ui*.

The term *fei-ts'ui*, which literally means kingfisher feathers, was current up until the Sung dynasty (A.D. 960-1279) as a name for dark green nephrite of the finest quality. After falling into disuse, except when referring to feathers, it reappears at the end of the eighteenth century to describe jadeite.

Although jade carving is one of the arts most closely associated with Chinese culture, and has been practised in China for more than 3,000 years, it still presents many problems to the student of technology and art history. The most prominent of these is that of assigning dates to jades made after the period of the Han dynasty (206 B.C. — A.D.220). The first scientific archaeological expedition in China was carried out by the Historical Society of the Academia Sinica, from 1929 to 1933, on the site of the Shang dynasty metropolis of Anyang. Since then, and especially during the period from 1949 until the present, excavations have been carried out over a large area of China and have yielded sufficient material for us to be able to build up a picture of the culture of the people from prehistoric times until the third century A.D., a period stretching back almost as far before the birth of Christ as we are after it. These excavations have produced a number of jade objects, and from these objects a clear picture of the origins and development of the jade carvers' art can be formed.

After the Han dynasty, however, the problem of dating becomes more difficult. Very little scientific excavation of sites from the Six Dynasties period (A.D. 265 — 587) until the Ch'ing dynasty (A.D. 1644 — 1912) has been attempted, and the little that has been done has not been fully published. Hence there is no pattern of stylistic change, such as we have for the earlier periods, to be used for comparison. Nothing at all concerning the date of carving can be learnt from the stone itself: it is relatively speaking all of the same age in geological time. The method employed by western scholars for dating jade carving is by comparing the jade object with works of art in other media; for example, stone and wood sculpture, bronze, pottery and lacquer, so that the style of a piece can be related to the general artistic feeling of a particular period. This method has a number of disadvantages, but it at least provides a basis on which to work.

2 BRONZE KUEI

The main difficulty is caused by the conservative Chinese approach to art and decorative patterns from ancient times, notably from the period of the bronzes of the Shang and Chou dynasties. As can be seen by comparing the jade vessel in plate 18 with the bronze *kuei* in figure 2 'copying' one form from the other may be carried out exactly; or the jade may be adapted from a bronze shape, for example the incense burner of the altar set shown in plate 26, which is adapted from a bronze shape called a *ting*, and the two vases on either side of this which are adapted from a bronze *ku*. The two periods chiefly associated with this archaic style are the Sung dynasty (A.D. 960 — 1279) and the Ch'ing dynasty (A.D. 1644 — 1912), especially the period of the late seventeenth and eighteenth centuries. It is generally considered that more accurate copies in jade of the early bronzes are likely to date from the Sung dynasty, while craftsmen of the later period tended to incorporate archaic motifs into their own decorative schemes (for example the decoration on the rhyton or ritual vessel in plate 33), and to adapt shapes rather than copy them exactly. But there is no reason why an eighteenth-century jade carver should not have copied, as exactly as his technique would allow, an archaic bronze.

The other fact that must be taken into consideration is the use of pebbles and boulders of jade for carving so that as little of the material as possible is wasted, and so that the

14

shape and colour of the finished carving should follow closely that of the original piece of jade. This applies to the enormous number of naturalistic carvings of animals, ranging in size from small objects like the camel in plate 14, to the large buffalo in plate 20. This buffalo has become famous, not only as a masterpiece of jade carving but also for the number of different periods to which it has been attributed. It is said to have been attributed to the Han dynasty in a catalogue of the contents of the Winter Palace in Peking, compiled before 1900. It was also given this date in two exhibitions, in 1915 and 1935 — 36, after it had come to England. The attribution was then changed to early Ming dynasty, probably because a number of other buffaloes, none of them as large or as fine as this, had been given a date in the Ming period (A.D. 1368 — 1644). For the exhibition of the *Arts of the Sung Dynasty* held in 1960 by the Oriental Ceramic Society, this buffalo was given a Sung attribution (A.D. 960 — 1279). This appears to have been because this piece of sculpture 'exemplifies the inner character almost of a living beast', suggesting that this 'inner' quality was more likely to have been sought after and achieved by a Sung artist.

Very few references to the jade carver's craft are to be found in Chinese literature. For the most part the literary classes were indifferent to anything connected with manual labour, and ancient jades rarely, if ever, bore inscriptions for scholars to translate and discuss. Also, the craftsman himself was probably reluctant to divulge the secrets of his trade. In almost all cases the jade carvers worked without their identity being recorded. Some exceptions to this occurred during the Ming dynasty when occasional references to specific jade carvers are to be found; this is due probably to the fact that they had had a good education and had come into contact with the literati. The most famous of these Ming craftsmen was Luh Tzu-kang, who was also a painter and calligrapher and is said to have worked only with mutton fat jade. He established his workshop at Su-chou one of the great cultural centres in China. There are, however, in existence no pieces of jade that can be definitely attributed to Luh Tzu-kang.

The process of making an object possessing some artistic and aesthetic merit from a pebble or roughly cut block of jade is one of slow patient grinding, using as a medium an abrasive that is harder than jade. In this way it is not cut as the word 'carving' implies. The Chinese call this process *cho* and *cho mo*, but there is no satisfactory single word for it in English. The word 'carving' is used rather as suggesting the final result than the way it is obtained.

The modern Chinese jade carver has five different abrasive media to choose from: these are quartz sand, crushed almandine garnets, corundum, carborundum and diamonds. As well as these, there is the polishing medium called *pao yao*, 'precious powder'.

All these media, with the exception of the diamond are used in the form of fine sand and can be obtained in a number of different grades. One of these abrasives is applied to the surface of the jade after it has been wetted with water; the container filled with the abrasive can be seen at the right hand end of the bench in the frontispiece. In earlier times grease, called 'toad grease', was used to hold the sand on the surface of the jade. This name appears to be merely an expression for describing certain oily substances, rather than something produced by a toad. This gave rise to the misconception that the grease softened the jade so that it could be cut more easily.

Quartz sand was probably the abrasive used by the Neolithic people of China for carving jade, for it had the advantage of being readily available in large quantities, and of a quality ready for use. Such quartz sand is either pure silica or silicon dioxide (with a hardness corresponding to 7 on the Mohs Scale) and is called *huang sha*, meaning 'yellow sand'. It is, in fact, very little used today, and then only as a polishing medium in conjunction with the wooden polishing wheel.

Crushed almandine garnets, which are called *hung sha*, meaning 'red sand', have a hardness of $7^{1}/_{2}$. Chemically they are silicates of calcium and iron. This medium probably came into use about the tenth century A.D., but it may have been used as early as the T'ang dynasty (A.D. 618 — 906). The garnets are brought to the sand warehouse in the form of coarse grains which are reduced to finer particles by a millstone pulled by a donkey, the crushed garnets are then sieved and the larger particles returned for re-grinding.

Next in order of increasing hardness, is black corundum or emery. This is made up of oxides of aluminium and iron ground in large mortars. In so far as the natural substances used by the jade carvers are concerned, it is only less hard than the diamond, being 9 on the Mohs Scale. This was probably first used during the Chin dynasty (A.D. 1115 — 1234) or the Yuan dynasty (A.D. 1280 — 1368).

In modern times, corundum has been largely superseded by a synthetic material, carborundum. This is a crystalline form of silicon carbide and is called *hei sha*, or sometimes *kuang sha*, 'Canton sand' to distinguish it from corundum. It was first imported into China through Canton. It has a hardness of $9^{1}/_{2}$ and was first produced in the U.S.A. in 1891. Before the second World War it was imported into China from the U.S.A., Sweden, or Japan. Although it is more expensive than the other abrasives used, it is preferable to them because of its greater hardness and the fact that it can be obtained in a more accurately graded state. Carborundum first came into use for jade carving some time between 1919 and 1939.

The diamond, called *chin-kang shih* by the Chinese, is the hardest of the natural minerals on the Mohs Scale, where it has a value of 10. The diamond is used in the form

16

of splinters fixed on to the head of a drill. It was originally used only for specialised work, for example the cutting of inscriptions, but in recent times power-driven diamond saws have been used for cutting blocks of jade. The chief use of the diamond is as a drill prior to open-work carving.

The polishing medium is called *pao yao*, meaning 'precious powder'. It is a fine grey powder and its composition has been established by Professor Hansford from samples collected by him in Peking in 1939. *Pao yao* consists of a mixture of a small quantity of carborundum (sometimes in more than one grade) with earth of the type of loess. Loess is the silt carried down by the Yellow River and deposited on the plains of its central and lower reaches. Before the introduction of carborundum the *pao yao* was probably made up by diluting corundum in the same way. It has been suggested that this 'precious powder' was jewel dust, crushed rubies and sapphires of gem quality, but this would have been far too costly. The process involved in producing corundum in powder fine enough for use in this way would have been sufficiently difficult and laborious to warrant the use of the word 'precious'. The presence of carborundum in the polishing medium accounts for the high gloss that is a characteristic of the surface of modern jades.

The following account of the processes of carving jade is intended only as a survey of the work involved. It is taken chiefly from the detailed account published by Professor S. Howard Hansford, in *Chinese Jade Carving*, based on his observations made in Peking during 1938 and 1939. The two illustrations, the frontispiece and figure 3, are taken from *Investigations and Studies in Jade: The Heber R. Bishop Collection*, published privately in two volumes in 1906 in New York. The first volume contains articles by a number of writers on the history of jade carving, the methods used and a scientific investigation of the nature of jade. The second volume consists of a catalogue of Mr. Bishop's collection, the greater part of which is now in the Metropolitan Museum, New York. This is one of the most remarkable books ever produced. Each volume measures $24^3/_4$ in. by 19 in. and the two weigh 125 lbs. One hundred copies were printed and distributed 'to all nations, in order that, through their public libraries, the scholar and writer may find them available for reference.' As part of Volume I, Mr. Bishop commissioned a Chinese artist to make a series of 100 sets of twelve paintings showing the various steps in carving a piece of jade. The sixth and a detail of the first of these are reproduced here.

Large blocks of jade are sawn up in the way shown in figure 3. All the other processes involved, including the removal of the 'skin' of pebbles and small boulders, are carried out on a bench like the one shown in the frontispiece. The preliminary work of cutting up the piece of crude jade or removing the 'skin', is done with a saw made of a single

3 METHODS OF CARVING JADE (detail)

strand of wire held taut by a bamboo frame. The cut is kept continually wet by a mixture of 'black sand' and water. All the jade carver's tools are made of steel or wrought iron, supplied by blacksmiths who specialise in the production of tools for this industry.

The first step in the production of a piece of jade carving is usually the making of a design by the head of the workshop. This may be his own design or taken from a book of patterns. Or, instead of using a design, the jade carver may prefer to take his inspiration from the piece of jade, making allowance for its shape and colour, so that as little as possible of the stone is wasted. During the long labour that follows, the various kinds of work are divided among a number of people, one man usually specialising in one particular stage or decorative feature in the production. Throughout the process of carving the jade, the worker's eyes are protected by bamboo screens, which can be seen over the top of the polishing wheels in the frontispiece.

The piece of jade is first cut to the approximate shape of the required object. This is done with steel discs of varying sizes. The disc is fixed to the end of a shaft which is rotated by means of a treadle. The jade is held in one hand and the wet abrasive is applied with the other. All the time he is working, the craftsman continually replenishes the wet 'sand' in the cut. If a large piece of jade is being carved, this can be suspended

18

from a beam with a counterpoise at the other end. All the rough edges left at the end of this stage are smoothed away using grinding wheels of various sizes.

If a design is being used, this is now drawn onto the jade with Chinese ink. The piece then passes to various workmen who execute this design using drills, the wire saw and grinding wheels. The designer follows the work closely through all its stages.

It is by means of the variety of drills at his disposal that the incredible tours-de-force produced by the jade carver can be achieved. For example, ring handles, such as those on the bowl in plate 30, swinging handles such as the one in plate 27, and even complete chains, all cut without a break from a single piece of jade can only be produced by the patient and ingenious use of drills. These are also used to produce decoration in relief, a good example of this being the all-over decoration of dragons and waves on the bowl in plate 21. If open-work carving is required, the area is first drilled through and through, then the unwanted section is cut away, using the wire saw. The rough edges, again, would be smoothed away with the grinding wheels. An example of particularly complicated open-work can be seen in the twisted stems that support the lotus leaf vase in plate 35.

Sometimes a bottle with the hole in the neck narrower than the interior of the body, is required. This is done by drilling with an open tubular drill so that the core of the piece of jade can be removed. The interior is then enlarged by means of gouges and an abrasive. The act of removing the core, which is done by breaking it off as far down as possible, is one requiring great skill.

When the final shape of the object has been obtained it is then ready for polishing. Again wheels of different sizes are used, made from wood or several layers of leather or, for more inaccessible areas, small plugs cut from a gourd. The *pao yao*, made into a paste with water, is spread over the surface of the wheel. A number of polishing wheels can be seen on the shelves behind the two workers who are using the wooden and leather polishing wheels, in figure 2. If the jade carver cannot achieve the gloss he requires by the use of polishing wheels, this may sometimes be simulated by applying a coat of wax which is then polished.

Before the first century B.C., Chinese historians, writing under the influence of Confucian teaching made no allowance for prehistory, and there is no such term in ancient Chinese literature. Confucian philosophy required that at all times the government of China should be in the hands of a single emperor. Lists of these emperors, some with incredibly long lives, were drawn up and based on myths common at the time. One account of the history of this period tells of three epochs. The first two were called the Epoch of the Three Emperors and the Epoch of the Five Emperors. During this period the world was set in order and man was raised from a state of barbarism to the beginning of civilisation. The third period, called the Epoch of the Three Dynasties marks the point after which tradition can be tested against archaeological data. The three dynasties are called the Hsia, the Shang and the Chou. The Hsia dynasty still remains shrouded in mystery, but the Shang and Chou periods are known to have existed and archaeologists have collected a great deal of information about them.

The Shang dynasty is now regarded by archaeologists as the first historic period. This was preceded by a number of cultures ending with the Neolithic age. A number of polished hardstone implements and other objects, including some in jade have been excavated from Neolithic sites. The jade objects include *hüan*, *yüan* and *pi* discs pendants, axes, chisels and arrow-heads and a highly stylised figure of a bird. In order to carry out the carving, sandstone slabs were used as grinding tools and the surface was polished with sand. A number of different types of drill must have been in use during this period, including a hollow tubular drill. Small holes were made by drilling with a thin piece of bamboo and fine sand. Some facts about the methods of carving, polishing and drilling used by the Neolithic people in China may be deduced from the methods used by the Maoris of New Zealand, who lived in a stone age society, at least until the middle of the nineteenth century. One of the characteristic features of their culture was the use of jade for pendants, weapons and tools.

During the Neolithic period the foundations were laid of the subsequent Chinese culture. The term *Neolithic* is used here only in a cultural sense, because some groups of Stone Age people continued to flourish after the beginning of the Shang dynasty and the discovery of metals.

The traditional dates for the Shang dynasty are 1766 B.C. to 1122 B.C. These dates have been questioned in modern times and one widely accepted theory, made after a study of inscriptions on oracle bones, sets them at 1751 and 1111 B.C. respectively. It is best to treat them as approximate until further evidence comes to light.

No contemporary records of the Shang dynasty have survived, the earliest literary accounts of this period dating from the following Chou dynasty. These accounts have been considerably supplemented by archaeological data.

The Shang people occupied an area in China confined to the territory consisting of the central and lower plains of the Yellow River. This area is called by Chinese historians the Central Plain. Shang society was organised on a feudal basis, with two distinct levels — the warrior nobility and the common people. The dynasty is known to have had seventeen generations of rulers, who moved their capital six times. The most important achievements of this period include the invention of bronze and methods of bronze casting, the use of the chariot, the development of writing and the setting up of jade carving as a separate branch of the stone carving industry.

The Shang jade carver at first followed the techniques used by the Neolithic craftsmen. With the introduction of metals, he was able to add the wire saw to the short list of his utensils. This was used with sand as an abrasive for cutting up large blocks of jade, probably in much the same way as is shown in figure 3. Most of the jade implements of this period are well shaped and highly polished. Grooves and ridges, like the ones on the end of the blades in plate 1, show how far his skill had developed.

Smaller objects were sometimes decorated with geometric patterns produced by scratching, or with drills. The two methods most frequently used for producing lines are called *yin-wen*, depressed lines, and *yang-wen*, raised lines. It takes two of the depressed lines to make a raised line. An example where both these techniques can be seen is the fantastic bird in figure 4, the major part of the decoration is done with raised lines and the divisions of the beak and the claws are done in depressed lines.

The Shang jade carver used both large and small rotary tube drills as well as simple bamboo drills for making small holes. The holes may have been drilled right through from one side, or by drilling first on one side and then the other.

Jades made during this dynasty may be classified into three groups, according to their function. These are tools and weapons, ornaments, and ceremonial and religious objects.

The tools and weapons include objects such as axes, chisels, knives, spear-heads (plate 2) and arrow-heads. Some of these may also have served a ceremonial function.

Shang ornamental jades are mainly objects in the shape of animals for use as pendants or for fixing to some background material, such as wood or textiles. The animal carvings

4 FIGURE OF A BIRD

shown in plates 3 and 4 are of this type. The use of animal forms as decorative patterns is one of the outstanding features of Shang art. A composite animal form that occurs in Shang jades is the *t'ao t'ieh* mask. This mask is one of the most important decorative motifs used in Chinese art, and exists in a variety of forms. It may consist of a full-face mask of a single animal or it may be formed by two confronting animals with their heads placed close together in profile so that the features form a full-face mask. The use of this mask as a decorative element on later jades can be seen on the rhyton in plate 33. Another version of this mask can be seen in the band round the upper edge of the jade *kuei* in plate 17.

Great importance has been attached to ceremonial and religious paraphernalia during the Shang dynasty and all the following periods in Chinese history until the end of the Ch'ing dynasty in 1912. Often this was made from jade. The names given to these various ceremonial objects by later scholars have been taken from two classical Chinese texts, the *Chou-li* or Book of Chou Ceremony, and the *Li-chi* or Notes on Ceremony. These have been attributed to the Chou period, but were assembled and edited during Han times. Both contain later interpolations. All the shapes that are mentioned as being part of the Chou ritual and for burial of the dead, are to be found in the Shang period. The six most important of these emblems are the *pi*, the *ts'ung*, the *kuei*, the half *kuei* or *chang*, the *hu* and the half *pi* or *huang*. A number of theories have been put forward about the significance of the first three of these objects, but very little is known about the identification of the last three.

The *pi* disc is thought to be the symbol of heaven, a statement probably first made in the second century A.D. in a commentary on the *Chou-li*. This disc has a central circular opening about one-third of the total diameter. It is thought that this disc either represents the solar disc, or that the circular opening represents the sun shining in heaven. Its function in Chinese art has been described as being 'somewhat analogous to the cross-form' in western art. Other jade ring forms are called *hüan* if the opening has a diameter half that of the disc, and *yüan* if the opening is even wider. Examples of these three discs dating from late Chou and Han periods are shown in plate 6. The two magnificent *pi* discs in plates 8 and 11, show to what extent the later periods elaborated this simple shape with decoration.

The significance of the *ts'ung* is still doubtful. It is generally accepted that it is the symbol of the earth. It consists of a circular opening in a rectangular vessel. The outer surface is either left plain or divided into sections. It has been suggested that the *ts'ung* may originally have served some practical purpose during the Shang period and its symbolic use to represent the Earth may not have developed until the time of the adoption of the specific cult of an Earth deity, alongside that of Heaven, some time towards the end of the Chou period. The main body of Shang jades are cut from narrow blocks of jade and are two-dimensional in character. The *ts'ung* and a number of small animal carvings in the round are exceptions to this. The *ts'ung* shown in figure 5 dates from the ninth to the seventh century B.C.

The jade tablet called a *kuei* is thought to be a symbol of the east and has been identified with objects of the type shown in plate 9. *Kuei* were carved as sceptres and vary considerably in shape, the type with a triangular end being known as a *ku kuei*.

A number of Shang jades made in the shape of useful objects must have been used only for ceremonial purposes, probably to be carried as badges of rank. The two blades in plate 1 belong to this type. They are much too thin and hence too fragile ever to have been of use as cutting blades.

The Shang people were overcome by the Chou in about 1111 B.C. This conquering race had been living side by side with the Shang, like a number of other non-Shang people, possibly as a feudal state. The dynasty they established is divided by historians into two periods, the Western Chou dating from about 1111 B.C. until 771 B.C, when the capital then moved to Lo-Yang, in Honan. The dynasty then becomes known as the Eastern Chou, and this lasted until 222 B.C.

The Eastern Chou period is itself divided into two periods. The first of these dating from 722 to 481 B.C. is known as *Ch'un Ch'ui* or the period of the 'Spring and Autumn Annals'. These 'Annals' were a chronicle of the state of *Lu* and have at times been attributed to Confucius himself. The later part of this period was marked by political disorder and social disintegration. It is known as the period of the Warring States (about 481—221 B.C.).

The Chou dynasty lasted for a period of about 1000 years, the longest dynastic period in China's history. The Chou people formed a minority ruling group surrounded by a number of independent or partly independent tribes. The Chou feudal system, based on the early Shang system, was planned to give Chou people fiefs over a wide area. At the height of their power, the Chou people ruled an area covering the entire Yellow and Yangtze River basins. The result of this was a culture based on a number of influences.

At first the influence of the conquered Shang race was the strongest, but by the beginning of the second part of the Eastern Chou period, the mixture was complete and Chou China emerged as a cultural entity. This cultural unity existed before the physical unification of the empire of the Ch'in in 222 B.C.

During the Eastern Chou period there arose the various systems of Chinese philosophy and ethics, that were to influence not only Chinese culture in the years to come, but all the countries of the Far East. The most famous of these philosophers was Confucius, who was born in 551 B.C. in the Chou feudal state of Lu, in the modern province of

5 TS'UNG

Shantung. His doctrine of filial piety and its extension to loyalty to the good ruler, was based on a study of the Shang system of government and ancestor worship. In spite of the upheavals during the Warring States period, the disciples and followers of the various philosophers flourished, and the age is sometimes referred to as the period of the 'Hundred Schools'.

The art of the Western Chou period was an extension of the arts of the Shang dynasty, and as with other cultural activities the Chou style did not emerge until the beginning of the Eastern part of the dynasty. Just as the art of bronze casting reached its greatest heights during the Shang dynasty, the golden age of the jade carver was achieved during the Eastern Chou period. The use of the rotary cutting wheel was fully developed, and the first use of the diamond drill was probably made at this time. The Chou jade carver had, in fact, by this time all the tools that were used by his successors until the advent of modern power-driven equipment.

The use of jade for ceremonial and religious purposes carried on from the Shang dynasty. The type of jade object and its position in the tomb, for burial with the dead, was rigidly prescribed, and large numbers of mortuary jades have been excavated. These include *pi* discs, *ts'ung* squares, and *kuei* sceptres.

Lists of excavated jades from Eastern Chou sites show that tools and implements are rarely found, and that jade was increasingly used for ornamental purposes. The technical advances made during this time went hand in hand with an increase in interest in the quality of the material and in the surface decoration. The complexity and variety of objects discovered show that the jade carver could produce anything his customers required.

Typical Chou surface patterns are to be seen in the squared spiral decoration on the two plaques in plate 5, and the grain pattern on the *pi* discs in plate 6 and plate 8. The 'grain' pattern is so called because the small round projections incised with a small spiral resemble the new shoots on a wheat grain. The complex arrangement of fabulous bird motives and the corn pattern separating the two bands of decoration on the *pi* disc in plate 10 appear towards the end of this period and continue into the Han dynasty.

A number of elaborate pendants made up of interlocking parts carved from single pieces of jade show the amazing skill of these jade carvers. In the British Museum is a chain of four discs, connected by links, carved from a pebble less than nine inches long.

Jade was used for making musical chimes for use on state or religious occasions. Writings were sometimes inscribed on jade tablets, and jade seals appear for the first time.

The magnificent disc in plate 8, carved with two 'heraldic' lions on the outer edge, is one of the finest and most beautiful of all the jades dating from the Warring States period. The complexity of the design, coupled with great freedom of execution are an indication of the heights which the jade designer and carver had reached at this time.

The troubled period of the Warring States was brought to an end with the supremacy of the state of Ch'in in 221 B.C. The Chou feudal system of government was destroyed and a central government with an emperor at its head set up in its place. The king of Ch'in took the title *Ch'in Shih Huang Ti*, 'the First Emperor of the Ch'in dynasty'. The most notable survival of his reign is the Great Wall, formed by joining together and extending a number of earlier walls. His reign is also said to have been marked by the famous 'burning of the books', carried out as part of his attempt to wipe out the memory of the previous age. After his death, the Ch'in dynasty survived less than eight years, before it was overthrown. In 206 B.C., Lui Pang ascended the throne as the first emperor of the Han dynasty. This dynasty, except for the period A.D. 9—22 when the throne was in the hands of the usurper Wang Ming, survived for four centuries.

The Han emperors, with their capital at Ch'ang-an (modern Sian) pursued a policy of territorial expansion. Chinese ambassadors during the reign of the Emperor Wu Ti (141—87 B.C.) brought China, for the first time, into direct contact with the western world. This westward drive resulted in the opening of the Old Silk Road across central Asia. This was to have considerable effect on both the commercial and cultural interests in China.

By this route, silk was exported from China and exchanged for a variety of products including ponies, spices and jade. It was probably during this period that Khotan jade was first used by Chinese lapidaries. In A.D. 65 the Buddhist doctrine was introduced into China from India. This was to have a momentous effect on the subsequent art of China and, indeed, on Chinese civilisation as a whole.

Excavations on the sites of outposts set up to maintain the Empire have revealed a clear picture of the arts of the Han period. These sites are as far apart as Korea and Chinese Turkestan, Northern Mongolia and Vietnam, as well as a number of sites in both north and south China.

The changes that occurred in social and religious conditions resulted in a change of emphasis from the ancient ritual procedures to an interest in secular objects and activities. The increase in the number of objects in jade, made for secular use, first noticed towards the end of the Chou period, continued during the Han. The production of certain ritual jades, notably the *pi* disc was carried on throughout this period. The use of two dimensional decorative patterns gradually began to be superseded by an interest in three dimensional carving.

The Han people took a great interest in horses. They appear as pottery or wooden figures for burial with the dead, and on funerary reliefs in clay and stone. The Emperor Wu-ti

was so fascinated by the fabulous horses reported to be bred in Bactria and Sogdiana, that he undertook the conquest of these countries to obtain them. The magnificent jade head and shoulders of a horse, in the Victoria and Albert Museum (plate 11) has been attributed to the Han dynasty by stylistic comparison with the pottery and wooden grave figures.

Jade seals with animals carved on the top, first make their appearance during this period. A number of stylised figures of pigs, possibly used as shroud weights, have been excavated from Han sites. Objects for decorating a sword and its scabbard were made and a sword slide similar to the one in plate 7, has been excavated from the site of Lo-lang, a Han outpost in Korea. Jade decorative objects for personal adornment include pendants and belt hooks and jade was used as inlay on bronze objects, as can be seen on the belt hook in figure 6.

After the re-establishment of the dynasty in A.D. 22, the capital was moved from Ch'ang-an to Lo-yang. The dynasty continued until A.D. 220, when the empire was divided into three — the period from 221 until 265 is known as *San Kuo*, the Three Kingdoms. The Three Kingdoms period lasted until 265 and was succeeded by an even more complicated division of the country into Northern and Southern dynasties, each divided into smaller states. In 581 the Empire was again united by the Sui dynasty. Just as the Han dynasty was preceded by the short-lived Ch'in period, the Sui dynasty, which survived only 37 years, was the prelude to the great T'ang dynasty.

No jades of the period from 220 until the beginning of the Sui dynasty have been excavated in China. The jade water vessel in the shape of a fabulous animal in plate 12 is similar to one that has been attributed to this period by comparison with similar shaped objects in ceramic material and bronze, and sculpture in stone. Two tombs of the Sui dynasty that can be dated 581 and 610 have revealed a number of jade plaques, but no other jades have been attributed to this period.

The rulers of the T'ang dynasty, building on the unity bequeathed by the Sui, were able to increase China's territories and influence to an extent comparable with that of the Han. T'ang rulers welcomed foreigners to their capital at Ch'ang-an. The T'ang empire reached its greatest heights around A.D. 750 and a period of decline followed.

At least five tombs have been opened containing jades dating from the T'ang dynasty, or from areas where T'ang influence continued after the fall of imperial rule. The most important of these is the tomb of Wang Ch'ien, a military commander who set himself up as 'emperor' of a southern area, between 907 and 918. The tomb contained two jade books, each made up of 53 leaves of white jade, with engraved and gilded characters. In the coffin were eight white jade plaques, each carved with a dragon that decorated the 'imperial' belt. There was also a jade disc engraved with a design of phoenixes and a jade

6 BRONZE BELT HOOK

seal. It has been suggested that these jades form a stylistic link between the jade carvings of the T'ang and Sung dynasties.

The black jade horse in plate 13 has been traditionally attributed to this period. In a catalogue of the contents of the Winter Palace in Peking, made before 1900, it was said to be of the Han dynasty but the general feeling at the present is that it is later than the T'ang dynasty.

In 906, the T'ang empire was succeeded by another period during which the country was divided, known as the period of the Five Dynasties. In 960 Chao K'uang-yin again united China, under the Sung dynasty. By comparison with the Han and the T'ang, the Sung empire was much smaller in size and the Sung people discovered a world of peace and refinement within their own borders. Their horizons were much reduced when in 1127 the court was forced to flee from the capital of K'ai Feng to the south, by the Kin, one of the nomad tribes from the Mongolian steppes. The new capital was set up at Hangchow. This Southern period of the dynasty lasted until 1279.

Sung dynasty art is characterised by a return to purely Chinese forms and a conscious attempt to imitate the art of earlier dynasties, especially the late Chou and early Han periods. Jade carving was probably influenced by monumental sculptures and by illustrated catalogues of archaic bronzes. The jade *kuei* in plate 17 attributed to this period appears to have been directly copied from an eleventh or twelfth-century B.C. bronze, or from an illustration of one of these bronzes. Other vessels have been given Sung dates, such as the libation vessel in plate 18.

A number of carvings of animals made from pebbles of jade, have been attributed to this period. Because of the vigour of its spirit, the camel, in plate 14, has been attributed to the early part of the period before all trace of the T'ang dynasty had passed away. This jade shows the carver's use of the 'skin' of the pebble as part of the decorative design.

The objects in the set of imperial paraphernalia in plate 16, carved in pure white jade are engraved with very finely drawn characters, which include dates corresponding to 1112 and 1124. These dates fall during the period of the Emperor Hui Tsung, the last emperor of the Northern Sung dynasty and to whom these tablets are thought to have belonged. The shapes of some of the objects are copied from archaic jades, for instance the *kuei* sceptre on the right is comparable with the *kuei* sceptre in plate 9.

By the year 1279, the Mongol tribes of the north had overrun the entire Sung empire and the Yüan dynasty was set up by Kublai Khan, a descendant of the great Genghis Khan. The Yüan emperors had their capital at Peking. During this dynasty the area under one ruler was the greatest in China's history.

Besides the interest in archaism so pre-eminent in the Sung dynasty, two new styles that were to become increasingly important began to make their appearance during the Yüan dynasty. One of these styles is predominantly naturalistic and includes bowls in the shape of fruit or flowers and vessels or 'mountains' of jade covered with scenes carved in high relief (see page 36). The second style is almost the opposite of this and tends to follow ceramic shapes with great emphasis on simple lines.

During the thirteenth century a more efficient abrasive than the crushed garnets—'red sand'—was introduced from the region of Ta-t'ung on the Mongolian border. This may have been the first use of the corundum—black sand—used in modern times. The increased cutting power enabled the jade carver to produce a number of large carvings. A large jade bowl is mentioned by a Franciscan friar, the Blessed Oderic of Pordenone, who made a missionary journey to China in the early fourteenth century. This bowl has been identified with a bowl restored to the Imperial collection by the Emperor Ch'ien-lung in the eighteenth century, is $23^1/_2$ in. (59.5 cm.) high and has a diameter of up to $51^1/_2$ in. (130.2 cm.). The outside of the bowl is carved with dragons swimming among waves. This was copied later on a number of bowls (see plate 21). Other large jade carvings known to have existed by the fourteenth century were jade mountains, and large stones for use as gongs.

The magnificent large jade buffalo in plate 20, that has been attributed to the Han, Ming and Sung periods at various times, may well have been made during the fourteenth century. At this time the jade carver would have had the kind of abrasive necessary to cope with an object of this size. Numerous other buffaloes of this type, usually rather smaller, have been attributed to later Ming periods and on into the eighteenth century.

An interesting comparison can be made between a group of porcelain cup stands with scalloped edges and a bowl in the Fitzwilliam Museum (plate 19). These cup stands, either undecorated or with underglaze blue or red decoration, have been conclusively attributed to the fourteenth century. There is also a silver cupstand in the British Museum of the same shape that is datable to the Yüan dynasty. It is tempting to use these as a means of dating this jade bowl, with the same shaped edge, to the same period.

The first Ming emperor, who took the title Hung-wu, was a native Chinese, and the establishment of the Ming dynasty was a triumph over foreign invaders. Hung-wu reigned from 1368 until 1398 and the dynasty he set up ruled China until 1644. A great many jade carvings have been attributed to the Ming period, but in fact, the number that can be definitely dated within these 300 years, is very few.

Two Chinese jade cups that once formed part of the collection given by the Persian Shah Abbas to the shrine of his ancestors at Ardebil in 1611 are now in the Archaeological Museum in Teheran. Hence they can be dated to the late sixteenth or early seventeenth centuries. Unfortunately the quality of the carving of these cups is rather poor, but they do represent types found elsewhere.

The most notable jades that have been excavated from a Ming site are those found in the tomb of the Emperor Wan-li, who was buried in 1620. They include vessels and jewellery of the highest quality. Jade objects and jewellery have also been discovered in the tombs of concubines of Wan-li and of the Emperor T'ien-Ch'i, who reigned from 1621 until 1627.

China was again subjected to foreign domination in 1644 when the last of the Ming rulers was overcome by Manchu invaders from the north, and the Ch'ing dynasty was founded. This dynasty ruled China from 1644 until 1912. During the reign of the second Emperor, K'ang-hai (1662–1722), China was restored to the position of the most important power in the far east. From the end of the seventeenth century and throughout the eighteenth century, China enjoyed a period of political stability and great commercial prosperity. In spite of efforts to maintain their national identity, the Manchus accepted and were soon dominated by Chinese culture.

The decorative arts of this period reached a height of technical perfection, never before achieved in Chinese history. The jade carvings produced during this period are among the finest ever made. Nephrite, in large quantities was obtained from Chinese Turkestan until 1856, when the trade ceased with Khotan and Yarkand. Jadeite — *fei ts'ui* —from Burma was first imported into China during the eighteenth century.

The Emperor Ch'ien-lung (1736–1795) took an active interest in collecting jades. Jade carving workshops were set up within the precincts of the Palace in Peking. A number of pieces are known with imperial inscriptions and a date of this reign. These include a group of jade mountains — huge boulders of jade carved all over with landscapes in high relief. The 'mountain' in figure 7 is now in the Walker Art Gallery in Minneapolis, and bears the date 1784. The rhyton in plate 33 is inscribed and dated 1787.

An enormous number of ornamental jade carvings were made during the eighteenth century. These included such things as vases (plate 29), bowls (plate 31), jade flowers for miniature gardens, panels to be set into furniture, screens (plate 32), figures of men and women, and animals. A variety of objects for use on the scholar's writing table — such things as brush pots, water containers, paper weights and brush rests.

Just as during the Sung dynasty, great interest was expressed in the past, especially the period of the Han dynasty and before. One of the predominant styles in art during the Ch'ing dynasty involved the use of archaic motifs. It is generally thought that Ch'ing artists adopted a more formal and decorative attitude towards this archaism than their Sung counterparts.

Jade was used for religious and ceremonial paraphernalia and the Emperor used jade

7 JADE 'MOUNTAIN'

objects when making the seasonal sacrifices. Religious ceremonies were accompanied by music made on jade gongs.

After the fall of this dynasty and the establishment of the Republic in 1914, jade carvers were freed from many of the conventions that court patronage imposed on them. The removal of this patronage also meant that large pieces of jade carving were no longer ordered, a commercial loss that was counterbalanced to some extent by an increasing trade in jade jewellery with America and Europe.

PERSIA AND INDIA

The Mughal dynasty in India had its origins in central Asia. Baber, its founder, was a descendant of both Timur and Ghengis Khan. Mughal, which means the same as Mongol, strictly only applies to the narrow-eyed tribes of the Steppe lands, but in India it was used to distinguish all foreign Mohammedans originating from Central Asia. The ruler of India during this period was referred to by Europeans as 'The Great Mogul'.

Baber defeated the Sultan of Delhi, Ibrahim Lodi, at Panipat in 1526, only to lose his newly won possessions shortly after. The dynasty was not properly established until 1556, shortly before the reign of his grandson, Akbar. Akbar reigned from 1556 until 1605 and the Mughal empire and the style of Mughal court art originated under his rule. The greatest heights of territorial and cultural expansion were achieved during the reigns of Akbar's grandson, Jahangir (1605–1627) and Jahangir's successor Shah Jehan (1627–1658). Because of the splendour of the court during this period, India gained the reputation in Europe of being a land of untold riches.

Shah Jehan was held prisoner by his son during the later period of his life. This son, Aurungzeb, succeeded him in 1658 and reigned until 1707. The period of the dynasty's decline began during his reign. In 1739 Delhi was sacked by the Persian army, and Mughal rule never fully recovered from this blow. The dynasty staggered on and finally collapsed after the Indian Mutiny in 1857, during the period of British rule.

The art of the Mughal court was influenced by a number of styles. As foreign invaders, they were influenced by native Indian art, at the same time imposing their own Islamic traditions on their Indian subjects. Akbar did his best to attract craftsmen from abroad into his service, a policy also followed by Jahangir and Shah Jehan. Persians, Afghans, Arabs and Europeans are known to have worked for the Mughal emperors. European influence was greatest during the reign of Jahangir, mainly through Portuguese Jesuit missionaries and occasionally travellers, like William Hawkins.

Hawkins set out from England in 1607 in command of an East India Company ship, part of his mission being to carry letters and presents from James I to the 'princes and governors' of India. Hawkins arrived at the Mughal court in Agra in April 1609 and remained there for nearly three years. During his stay he became one of the Emperor's intimate friends. Hawkins died on the way back to England, but the journal he kept during his stay in India was eventually published. In this journal, Hawkins mentions five hundred jade wine cups.

As yet, very little is known about the origins and development of jade carving in

India. Before the beginning of Mughal rule, there does not appear to have been any jade carving at all. By the middle of the seventeenth century this industry was flourishing and produced some of the finest objects carved in jade anywhere in the world (plate 41).

The ancestors of the Mughals, the Timurid rulers of Persia, were certainly familiar with jade. A great monolith of dark green jade, used as a cover for the tomb of Timur (died 1405) is in the Gur Emir Mosque in Samarkand. Persian lapidaries are known to have carved rock crystal, a material that is harder than jade, and a small number of jade vessels have been attributed to Persian craftsmen. Included among these is the vessel in plate 38. There is an inscription carved round the neck of this jug which includes the titles of the Timurid ruler Ulugh Beg, that were adopted by him in 1417. Ulugh Beg died in 1449, so the jug can be dated to some time within these thirty-two years. This jug later passed into the possession of the Mughal emperor Jahangir, and from him to Shah Jehan. These Persian craftsmen probably accompanied the dynasty to India where the settled conditions and intellectual stimulation that prevailed during the late sixteenth and seventeenth centuries would account for the flowering of their art.

Baber and his descendants were great lovers of nature. They delighted in trees and flowers, and one of their favourite diversions was landscape gardening. Under Jahangir, careful studies of birds and animals and plants, executed by his order, are some of the most delightful products of Mughal painting. This attachment to animal and plant forms is one of the characteristic features of Mughal jades. Bowls in the shape of flowers (plate 41) or gourds (plate 39), birds-head handles (plate 40) and horses heads for dagger handles (plate 45) are all motifs favoured by these jade carvers.

Another feature of Mughal jade carving is the use of precious stones, gold or different coloured jade as inlaid decoration (plates 43, 44, 45,), often with quite striking effect.

Another theory put forward to explain the origin of Mughal jade is that Chinese jade carvers were among the craftsmen attracted to India by the Mughals. These jade carvers would have trained native workers, who were responsible for the establishment of the Islamic stylistic characteristics of Mughal jades. The answer may well be a combination of these two theories.

During the eighteenth century a number of Mughal jades aroused sufficient interest in China for the style to be copied there. It is extremely difficult to distinguish whether a particular jade carving is Mughal or Chinese in the Mughal style.

NEW ZEALAND

The two islands of New Zealand were discovered by Abel Tasman in 1642 and given this name a few years later by the Dutch. It was not until 1769 that Captain James Cook, sailing in the *Endeavour* rediscovered the islands and claimed them for the British crown. This act was disavowed by the Parliament of the day and New Zealand did not become a British possession until 1840. In the meantime parts of the islands were settled by whalers and traders.

Both Tasman and Cook encountered the natives of New Zealand, the Maoris. The ancestors of this Polynesian race arrived on the islands about the middle of the fourteenth century, the last of a number of waves of canoe voyagers. They remained in a stone-age environment at least until the European settlers arrived during the first half of the nineteenth century. All their weapons and tools were made from stone, shell, bone or wood, or jade. The jade is called by the Maoris *pounamu* and a number of their legends closely connect it with the discovery of the islands by their ancestors. Of all the centres where jade has been carved with any degree of skill, the work carried out by the Maoris is the least elaborate. There is quite a large amount of fairly detailed knowledge about its provenance and the methods used for carving it, but, once again, any accurate dating of the objects involved is extremely difficult.

The jade found in New Zealand is all nephrite. It is predominantly green in colour, ranging from very dark green through lighter shades to greyish green. Sir Joseph Banks, in his account of his visit to New Zealand with the *Endeavour*, mentions 'greenstone' ornaments worn by the natives, and this is the name given to it by the later European settlers. The best and most important works in jade appear to have been made on the North Island, but jade carving of varying degrees of skill was carved out on both islands.

The Maoris used jade for making both useful and decorative objects. The simplest things are adzes, axe-heads and chisels, to be used for making elaborate wood carvings and for finishing the slabs of wood lashed into their canoes as topsides. They also make long, narrow cylindrical jade pins for holding together the mats they wear as shawls. The flat, round-ended club, called a *mere* or *patu pounamu* (plate 47) was used both as a weapon and as a piece of tribal insignia. These *meres* have also been used as title-deeds for land, and many have been given names, usually that of the particular area with which they are associated.

Maori ornaments in jade consist of a variety of pendants. These were worn either suspended from the ear or round the neck. They range in shape from long plain cylinders to more elaborate fish pendants and *hei-tiki* (plates 46 and 48).

33

The curious shaped figure of the hei-tiki does not represent a god and is not worshipped as such. *Tiki* is the name given to the Polynesian equivalent of Adam, the first man, fashioned from red clay by the god *Tane*. The large carved, wooden figures on the gables of houses or set up near a house are also called tiki. *Hei* means suspended, *hei-tiki* being a *tiki* for wearing round the neck. They are used by the Maoris as mementoes of previous owners and are valued for their associations, and not for any considerations of size or beauty. The *hei-tiki* was usually buried with its owner when he died, and later retrieved. It was then used for reviving memories by his friends and relatives.

The piece of jade to be carved was first cut to the approximate size and shape of the object required. If a large piece of jade was to be cut to make a smaller object, it was cut from two sides and the pieces broken apart with a heavy blow before the cuts actually met. The cutting was carried out by continual rubbing with a piece of sandstone shaped like a blade, or by using a piece of wood and wet sand. The time taken to cut a $1\frac{1}{2}$– inch stone into the shape roughly that of a *mere* (plate 47) was about one month. The object was then slowly shaped and polished using wet sand as an abrasive. Sometimes this may have been done by taking the object down to the seashore and working with the sand there. For a *mere*, this took about six weeks. Most objects then had to be drilled. This was done using a piece of flint for the drill head, or using a piece of pounded wood with a little fine wet sand. Another tubular drill, perhaps made from a bone, must have been used for such things as marking the eyes of the *hei-tiki* (plate 46).

The Maoris also carved another green stone which can easily be mistaken for jade. This is called *bowenite* and belongs to the serpentine group of minerals. It is rather more translucent than jade with a slightly opalescent appearance. It has a hardness of 6 on the Mohs Scale.

The methods used by the Maoris for carving jade, working as they did entirely without the use of metals, can provide some ideas about the way in which other Neolithic people might have approached the various problems involved. This applies particularly to the jade carvers in China working before the introduction of metals.

PRE-COLUMBIAN AMERICA

A number of the native races that inhabited Mexico and Central America before the Spanish conquest in the early sixteenth century had lapidaries who were skilled as jade carvers. The jade they used was exclusively jadeite in the form of water-worn pebbles from alluvial deposits or mined in the highlands of Guatemala. The most highly developed of these jade carvers were to be found among the Olmec and Maya civilisations, and to a lesser degree by the Aztec people and the natives of the Costa Rican region.

The most notable works of art of the earliest civilisation, the Olmec (about 800–400 B.C.), have been found in a small area on the Gulf Coast, in the modern Mexican states of Veracruz and Tabasco. Small portable objects in Olmec style have been found in many other places in Mexico. The art of the Olmec people was dominated by a motive that combines the features of a jaguar with those of a human infant, known as a were-jaguar. At the great ceremonial centre of La Venta, have been found enormous heads and other sculpture in basalt, as well as objects in jade and serpentine. The style used by the jade carvers was derived from the monumental sculpture of this period. Jade objects in Olmec style include human and were-jaguar figures, pendants and masks. A were-jaguar mask is shown in plate 49, and appears to have been made to be worn.

The Maya Classic civilisation was preceded by the Proto-Classic period and is divided into the early Classic period and the Late Classic. At the height of this period, the people of the Maya civilisation were the most advanced of the Indian races in this area. They occupied the modern south eastern states of Mexico, British Honduras, the Peten district of Guatemala and Western Honduras. During the Classic period they built ritual centres which were not inhabited cities but extensive complexes of temples and pyramids. It has been suggested that Maya art has its technical and stylistic origins in painting and drawing which gives the Mayan sculpture a certain decorative flatness (plate 52). Sculptures in wood, stone, clay and jade were carried out by itinerant craftsmen, moving from one site to the next as demand required.

The jade was worked using sand as an abrasive and bone drills. The colour of the jade varies from a pale green stone to a bright apple green and a dark green.

The bas-relief style of carving can be seen in the beautiful plaque in plate 52. It shows a Maya dignitary seated on a throne, looking to his right and apparently addressing a small figure in the bottom left-hand corner of the plaque. The two circular objects, called flares, in plate 51 were made to be worn on the stretched ear-lobes. The limestone figure of the Maize God, from Copan, now in the British Museum (figure 8), shows this deity wearing ear flares of this type. This figure also wears a mask hanging round its neck, similar to the one shown in plate 53. The Pomona flare (plate 50) was found on the 'Pomona' fruit estates in Belize (formerly British Honduras) and is the largest of these circular ornaments yet discovered. Because of its great weight, it was probably made as a belt ornament or pendant. It dates from the Proto-Classic

3 LIMESTONE FIGURE OF THE MAYA MAIZE GOD

period and is decorated with incised glyphs — the elaborate Maya system of writing — that have not been interpreted. Jade was also used for making round and cylindrical beads, pendants and nose ornaments.

The Aztec empire arose in the fourteenth century and was centred on the Valley of Mexico and the island capital of Tenochtitlan. It spread outwards from the area to include most of the civilised people in Mexico.

The Aztecs produced enormous sculptures of gods and goddesses which made up their religious hierarchy. As with the Olmec and Maya jade carvers, the Aztec style was based on this sculpture (plate 54). The principal centre of the lapidaries' trade was Xochimilco. The material used was mainly in the form of small water-worn pebbles. The surface was polished, using an abrasive powder and bamboo fibres; drills were used with tubular bits of hardened copper.

The Spaniards conquered the Aztec empire and destroyed Tenochtitlan in 1521 and the jade looted from Mexico found its way, with other treasures, to Europe. The conquerors did not at first appreciate the high value which the Indians set on jade as a precious material and it may be that, in order to explain the Indians' reverence for it, the Spaniards imagined that there must have been healing properties in the stone which gave it its importance.

CHRONOLOGICAL TABLES

CHINA

Shang	1766–1122 B.C.
Chou	c. 1122–221 B.C.
Western Chou c. 1122–722 B.C.	
Eastern Chou (Spring and Autumn	
Annals Period) 722–481 B.C.	
Warring States period 481–221 B.C.	
Ch'in	221–207 B.C.
Han	206 B.C.–A.D. 221
Former (Western) Han 206 B.C.–A.D. 9	
Hsin (Wang Mang) A.D. 9–23	
Later (Eastern) Han A.D. 25–221	
Three Kingdoms	221–265
Six Dynasties Period	265–581
(Northern and Southern Kingdoms)	
Sui	581–618
T'ang	618–906
Five Dynasties	907–960
Sung	960–1279
Northern Sung 960–1126	
Southern Sung 1127–1279	
Yuan (Mongol)	1279–1368
Ming	1368–1644
Ch'ing (Manchu)	1644–1912
Republic	1912–1949
Peoples China	1949–
(Nationalist China or Formosa)	

INDIA Principal Mughal rulers

Baber	1526–1530
Humayun	1530–1556
Akbar	1556–1605
Jahangir	1605–1627
Shah Jehan	1627–1658
Aurangzeb	1658–1707

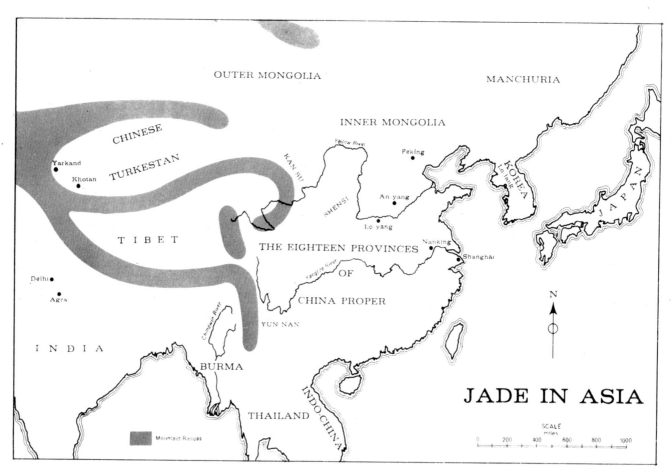

JADE IN ASIA

NOTES ON THE ILLUSTRATIONS

The dating of a number of the objects illustrated, especially between the Han and Ch'ing dynasties, is only provisional.

BLACK AND WHITE ILLUSTRATIONS

Frontispiece *Methods of carving jade.* Plates XII and XIII from *Investigations and Studies in jade: The Heber R. Bishop Collection*, Vol. I, New York, 1906.

These two illustrations show workmen polishing jade carvings. In the top section the workman is using a wooden polishing wheel. Immediately below this are shown two polishing tools adapted for polishing the interior of vases and bottles.

The lower section shows the leather polishing wheels, made by sewing together a number of layers of ox leather. The bench shown in these two illustrations was used throughout the carving process. The shield to protect the workman's eyes can be seen fitted over the wheel. The abrasive is shown in the container at the end of the bench.

Figure 2 *Bronze kuei.* About 10th century B.C. Height: 6½in. (16 cm.). China. Mount Trust, Churchill, Oxfordshire.

The shape and decoration of this bronze vessel should be compared with the jade *kuei* in plate 18.

Figure 3 *Methods of carving jade.* Detail of plate 1 from *Investigations and Studies in Jade: The Heber R. Bishop Collection*, Vol. I, New York, 1906.

This detail shows two workers cutting a block of crude jade with a wire saw. The pot hanging above the piece of jade contains water and the powdered abrasive is in the container on the ground beside the man on the right.

Figure 4 *Figure of a bird.* Shang dynasty (1766–1122 B.C.). Height: 5½ in. (14 cm.). China. British Museum, London.

There is a hole on the top right hand side of the crest of this bird (which is possibly an owl), that suggests that this object may have been used as a pendant. The major part of linear decoration on this bird has been produced by incising two lines close together to produce a central raised line. The beak and claws are marked using single incised lines.

Figure 5 Ts'ung. Shang dynasty (1766–1122 B.C.). Height: 8 in. (20 cm.). China. Victoria and Albert Museum, London.

Although the significance of the ts'ung is not at all clear, it is generally accepted as the symbol of the earth. See page 22.

Figure 6 *Bronze belt hook.* Han dynasty (206 B.C. A.D. 220). Length: 3³/₄ in. (9.5 cm.). China. British Museum, London.

This bronze belt hook has been inlaid with a panel of jade in the shape of a dragon.

Figure 7 *Jade 'mountain'.* 1784. Height: 23½ in. (60 cm.). Weight: 640 lbs. China. J. B. Walker Museum, Minneapolis.

On both sides of this 'mountain' are inscriptions by the Emperor Ch'ien-lung and a date corresponding to the year 1784. It formerly stood in the Summer Palace, outside Peking. Three other jade 'mountains', also dating from the eighteenth century, were reported in the Imperial Palace in Peking, in 1936. One of these was estimated to weigh at least seven tons.

Both Buddhists and Taoists have their paradises situated in the mountains and mountains were the abode of the Immortals. Jade has often been used to make representations of hills and mountains, usually carved from water worn pebbles — showing trees and streams, bridges and people in much the same way as the Minneapolis jade.

Figure 8 *Figure of the Maya Maize God.* Limestone. Height: 35 in. (89 cm.). Copan. British Museum, London.

In the ears of this figure, are shown flares of the type shown in plate 51. Also hanging round the neck of the figure is a mask similar to the mask in plate 53.

COLOUR PLATES

Plate 1 *Halberds.* Left: *small halberd (ko).* Shang dynasty (1766–1122 B.C.). Length: 8 in. (20 cm.). Right: *large halberd (ko).* Shang dynasty. Length: 12½ in. (31 cm.). China. Fitzwilliam Museum, Cambridge.

These two halberds are carved to such a degree of thinness that they would be of little use as defensive weapons. They were probably made to be carried as ceremonial paraphernalia. The pierced holes and serrations at the base indicate how these halberds were fastened to the shafts.

Plate 2 *Spear-head set in a bronze handle.* Probably Shang dynasty (1766–1122 B.C.). Length: 7³/₄ in. (19 cm.). China. British Museum, London.

This delicate white jade spear-head is still attached to the bronze and turquoise mount used for fixing it to the spear-shaft.

Plate 3 Left: *Cormorant holding a fish.* Shang dynasty (1766–1122 B.C.) or Western Chou period (1122–722 B.C.). Height: 1³/₄ in. (4 cm.). Right: *A Goose* (one of a pair). Probably Western Chou period (1112–722 B.C.). Height: 1½ in. (3 cm.). China. British Museum, London.

The small plaques in this plate and in plate 4 were made to be attached to some other material, possibly textile or wood. They were first produced in Neolithic times and continued until the Han dynasty.

It is interesting to note that the Chinese were using cormorants to catch fish at this very early date. The goose is a symbol of conjugal fidelity and usually appears in pairs.

Plate 4 *Stag and hind.* Left: *a stag.* Period of Warring States (481–221 B.C.) or Han dynasty (206 B.C.–A.D. 220). Height: 2¼ in. (5 cm.). Right: *a hind.* Period of Warring States (481–221 B.C.) or Han dynasty (206 B.C.–A.D. 220). Height: 1½ in. (3 cm.). China. British Museum, London.

The deer, in China, is a symbol of longevity and the small jade plaques representing stags are amongst the most fascinating produced during this period. These plaques show signs of burial as the surface of the jade is pitted and coarsened.

Plate 5 *Pair of plaques.* Period of Warring States (48–221 B.C.). Width: 6 in. (15 cm.). China. Fitzwilliam Museum, Cambridge.

These two plaques, representing fantastic creatures with their heads turned, looking over their backs, show the increasing interest in complicated shapes and whorled surface decoration that can be noticed during this Warring States period. The plaques show definite signs of having been cut from a piece of jade by a wire saw, and may have been made before the introduction of the rotary cutting disc.

Plate 6 *Three discs.* Left: *yüan.* Probably Han dynasty (206 B.C.–A.D. 220). Diameter: 4 in. (10 cm.). Centre: *pi.* Probably late Chou dynasty. Diameter: 5⁵/₈ in. (14 cm.). Right: *huan.* Warring States period (481–221 B.C.) or Han dynasty (206 B.C.–A.D. 220). Diameter: 4⁷/₈ in. (12 cm.). China. British Museum, London.

A Chinese glossary dating from the third or second century B.C. explains that if the jade is twice as wide as the perforation it is called *pi;* if the perforation is twice as wide as the jade it is called *yüan,* and if jade and perforation are of equal width it is called *hüa.*

Plate 7 *Sword furniture.* Top: *pommel* (?). Period of Warring States (481–221 B.C.) or Early Han Dynasty (206 B.C.–A.D. 220). Diameter: 1³/₄ in. (4 cm.). Left: *sword slide.* Han dynasty (206 B.C.–A.D. 220). Length: 3½ in. (8 cm.). Right: *scabbard chape.* Period of Warring States (481–221 B.C.). Height: 1½ in. (4 cm.). Bottom: *sword guard.* Period of Warring States (481–221 B.C.). Length: 2 in. (5 cm.). China. British Museum, London.

After the fall of the Shang dynasty, jade was used increasingly for making objects for personal adornment. Among the objects most frequently found are fittings made to decorate swords and scabbards, and various types are shown.

Plate 8 *Disc. (Pi).* Period of the Warring States (481–221 B.C.). Width: 8½ in. (21 cm.). China. Nelson Gallery, Atkins Museum, Kansas City. Nelson Fund.

This magnificent disc shows the degree of complication to which the jade carvers had carried the decoration of the simple *pi* shape. This object is made up of two discs, separated by a 'heraldic lion', with two similar lions on the outer edge.

Plate 9 *Sceptre. (Ku kuei).* Period of Warring States (481–221 B.C.) or early Han dynasty (206 B.C.–A.D. 220). Length: 8³/₄ in. (22 cm.). China. Victoria and Albert Museum, London.

The *kuei* sceptre was made in a number of forms, the shape shown in this plate being called a *ku kuei.* Such a sceptre was used by the Emperor when making sacrifices to the East. It is said to have symbolised 'spring and the first awakening of life'. A *ku kuei* was said to have accompanied the presents sent by the Emperor to his bride. *Kuei* sceptres were also badges of rank and were buried on the left-hand side of the body.

Plate 10 *Disc. (Pi).* Period of the Warring States (481 too 221 B.C.) or early Han period (206–220 B.C.). Diameter: 11 in. (27 cm.). China. Fitzwilliam Museum, Cambridge.

This *pi* disk is said to have been found at Chin-ts'un, a Chou period site in the city of Lo-yang, the capital of the Eastern Chou dynasty. It was discovered in 1928 having been excavated by the local inhabitants. Objects from the excavation were obtained through dealers and it is impossible to ascribe them to a particular tomb among the eight that were opened. The dates of the objects found in these tombs cover a period from 340 to 278 B.C.

Plate 11 *Head and shoulders of a horse.* Han dynasty (206 B.C.–A.D. 220) or later. Height: 7½ in. (19 cm.). China. Victoria and Albert Museum, London.

A number of pottery and wooden models of horses have

been recovered from Han burial sites, and the attribution of this famous jade horse is based on stylistic comparisons with these. Opinions are now inclining to a later date. Whatever the period this figure was carved, one can still be impressed by the strong features of the horse and the beautiful quality of the jade. See page 26.

Plate 12 *Water vessel in the shape of a winged feline monster.* Six Dynasties (A.D. 265–581) or later. Width: 4½ in. (11 cm.). China. Sir Alan and Lady Barlow, Wendover.

A jade animal similar to this water vessel has been attributed to the Six Dynasties period (265–581) on stylistic comparison with ceramic and bronze objects. This piece has also been attributed to the Sung dynasty (960–1279).

Plate 13 *A figure of a horse.* T'ang dynasty (A.D. 618–906) or later. Width: 10 in. (25 cm.). China. Fitzwilliam Museum, Cambridge.

This horse was carved from an exceptionally large piece of black and dark grey jade. It is said to have been attributed to the Han dynasty (206 B.C.–A.D. 220) in a catalogue of the contents of the Winter Palace in Peking, made before 1900. In the West it has been traditionally attributed to the T'ang dynasty (618–906) although there is no definite evidence to prove this. It may well have been carved at a later period. See note on plate 20.

Plates 14 and 15 *A figure of a camel.* Sung dynasty (A.D. 960–1279) or earlier. Width: 3½ in. (8 cm.). China. Victoria and Albert Museum, London.

The jade carver who made this camel from greenish-yellow jade has used the brown markings of the outer 'skin' of the pebble with considerable effect and economy. The vigorous style of this figure suggests that it may have been carved at an earlier period than the Sung dynasty.

Plate 16 *Set of Royal Tablets of the Emperor Hui Tsung* (A.D. 1082-1135) *of the Sung dynasty.* Probably made between 1112 and 1124. Length (of sword): 12½ in. (31 cm.). China. British Museum, London.

The pieces that make up this set of ceremonial objects are inscribed with poems and a shortened version of a Buddhist sutra in minute calligraphy. They also bear dates corresponding to the years 1122 and 1124. This period falls during the reign of the Sung Emperor Hui Tsung (1082–1135), the last emperor of the Northern Sung dynasty. The *kuei* sceptre (see plate 9) here appears as an object for ceremonial use.

Since there are no jades that can be definitely attributed to the Sung period, the date of these jades must remain open to question. An eighteenth-century date has been suggested for them. They have a wooden container which bears the seal of the Emperor Ch'ien-lung (1736–95).

Plate 17 *Vessel in the form of a* kuei *type bronze.* Sung dynasty (960–1279). Height: 3¾ in. (9 cm.). Width: 6¾ in. (17 cm.). China. Sir Alan and Lady Barlow, Wendover.

The type of bronze from which this jade was copied is shown in figure 2, and is called a *kuei.* The jade vessel reproduces the bronze almost exactly, without adapting any of the motives and hence is thought to be datable to the Sung dynasty (960–1279). See page 27.

Plate 18 *Libation cup.* Sung dynasty (960–1279) or later. Height: 4¾ in. (12 cm.). China. Fitzwilliam Museum, Cambridge.

The surface decoration on this vessel is carved in low relief in late Chou and Han style patterns, thought to be typical of Sung dynasty jades. See page 27.

Plate 19 *Jade bowl, with a porcelain cup stand.* Left: *cup stand.* 14th century. Diameter: 7¾ in. (19.5 cm.). Right: *jade bowl.* Possibly 14th century. 2¼ × 10 in. (5.5 × 25 cm.). China. Fitzwilliam Museum, Cambridge.

The method usually employed for the dating of the jade carvings after the end of the Han dynasty is generally one of stylistic comparison with objects in different media that can be more or less definitely dated, at the same time keeping in mind 'the distinctive spirit of each of these epochs'. A group of porcelain cup stands have been conclusively assigned to the Yuan dynasty (1280-1368). The circumference of these stands, as can be seen in this plate, is divided into eight pointed lobes. These clearly form a comparative basis for assigning the jade bowl, with its eight lobed rim, to the same period. This bowl has also been attributed to the earlier Sung dynasty (960–1279).

Plate 20 *A recumbent water-buffalo.* Possibly Yuan dynasty (1280–1368) or early Ming dynasty (1368–1644). Width: 17 in. (43 cm.). China. Fitzwilliam Museum, Cambridge.

In China, the bull was one of the signs of the Zodiac. In early times an ox was sacrificed to ensure the success of the crops, and sacrificed also to Heaven, Earth and the Imperial Ancestors.

This recumbent water buffalo is one of the masterpieces of Chinese jade carving. The artist has created a shape that involved wasting as little of the stone as possible. By a series of subtle curved lines the body of the buffalo has been made to appear soft to the touch—one almost expects to see its body rise and fall as it breaths. The carving of the buffalo's legs continues under its body.

This buffalo, together with the black horse (plate 13) and the *lung-ma* (plate 23) are said to have stood in a corridor in the Winter Palace in Peking. A catalogue of the contents of this palace attributed the buffalo and the horse to the Han period. They were brought to Peking by the Ming Emperor Yung-lo (1403–1425) and were regarded as sacred objects. They were used annually in a festival, perhaps because both the buffalo and the horse represent signs of the Zodiac. The Ch'ing Emperor, Kang-hsi (1662–1722) when inspecting the contents of the palace early in his reign is said to have asked how it was that the *lung-ma,* which brought the books of knowledge from out of the waves of the Yellow River was not represented. This was accordingly made and is that shown in plate 23.

These three pieces were removed from the Palace during the looting that followed the Boxer troubles in 1900.

Plates 21 and 22 *A bowl* with a view of the underside. Ming dynasty (1368–1644). Width: 12 in. (30.5 cm.). China. Private collection, England.

In his account of his stay in China the Friar Oderic of Pordenone, writing in the early fourteenth century, mentioned 'a great vessel of jade' that has been identified as one in the Palace Museum in Peking. This bowl was roughly circular in shape with a maximum diameter of 51½ in. (130.2 cm.) and 23½ in. (59.5 cm.) high. It was carved with dragons among waves, a design that was executed again on a number of smaller bowls. The bowl in this plate is a very fine example of this type, and the waves are continued under the bowl to form a whirlpool (plate 22). One of the dragon's heads can be seen on the right hand side of the edge of the bowl.

Plate 23 *Figure of a* lung-ma *(dragon horse)*. Possibly late 17th century. 5½ × 7¼ in. (14 × 18 cm.). China. Fitzwilliam Museum, Cambridge.

A *lung-ma* is a mythical beast with a dragon's body and horse's legs. It is shown here rising from the waves of the Yellow River carrying on its side the books of knowledge. This piece of jade is said to have been carved for the second Emperor of the Ch'ing dynasty, K'ang-Hai (1662–1722). See the note on plate 20.

Plate 24 *Standing figure*. Probably late 17th century. 12 in. (30.5 cm.). China. Sir Isaac and Lady Wolfson, London.

This figure was probably an attendant on some deity, perhaps *Shou Lao*, the god of longevity, or *Hsi Wang Mu*, the Queen Mother of the West. The bowl it carries was meant to contain an offering. The companion attendant figure is now in the Metropolitan Museum, New York.

Plate 25 *A set of ritual vessels for a Buddhist altar*. Late 17th or early 18th century. Height of candlestick without stand or pricket: 13 in. (33 cm.). Height of vases without stand: 11½ in. (29 cm.). Height of incense burner without stand: 10½ in. (26.5 cm.). China. Victoria and Albert Museum, London.

Ritual vessels of this type were made to be set up on the altar of a Buddhist shrine. This set consists of two pricket candlesticks (*chu t'ai*), two vases in the shape of *ku* bronzes and an incense burner in the shape of a *ting* bronze. The five pieces are carved from perfectly matched dark green jade. They are mounted on stands of gilt metal, decorated with cloisonné enamels.

Plate 26 *Jade book, made up of two green and five grey panels, with a wooden container*. 1748. Length of a single panel: 7³/₄ in. (19.5 cm.). Width of a single panel: 2³/₄ in. (7 cm.). China. British Museum, London.

The contents of this book consist of an essay on the Six Chinese Scripts. It bears a date corresponding to the year 1748.

Plate 27 *A vase and cover, with a swinging handle*. 18th century. Height with handle raised: 11½ in. (29 cm.). China. Mr G. de Menasce, O.B.E., London.

This beautiful white jade vase is distinguished by its purity of line and glowing translucence.

Plate 28 *Vase and cover*. 18th century. Height: 7 in. (17.5 cm.). China. Mr G. de Menasce, O.B.E., London.

The yellow jade used for making this vase is very rare and was much sought after. The smooth plainness of the body of the vase is in striking contrast with the formal decorations on either side.

Plate 29 *Vase and cover*. 18th century. Height: 9 in. (23 cm.). China. Mr P. D. Krolik, London.

The prototype for the shape of this vase is the pilgrim's water flask, designed to lie comfortably against the body when slung from the shoulder. This shape has been copied in bronze and porcelain as well as jade. It is sometimes called 'precious moon vase' by the Chinese.

The knop on the cover of this vase is carved in the shape of a dragon, and the handles are two phoenixes. One side, shown in this plate, is decorated with a prunus branch and rocks, and on the other side are growing carnations with rocks and fungus. The prunus is an emblem of flourishing old age, because it blossoms from leafless branches, before the winter is over.

Plates 30 and 31 *Bowl on four mask feet* with view of the interior. 18th century. Width: 9¼ in. (23.5 cm.). China. Mr P. D. Krolik, London.

This beautifully carved deep bowl has an intricate pattern of foliage inside (plate 30) and on either side, suspended from the mouths of beasts, two rings, carved from the same piece of jade as the bowl.

Plate 32 *Circular screen on a gilt bronze stand, decorated with cloisonné enamels*. Probably Ch'ien-lung period (1736–1795). Total height: 16 in. (40 cm.). China. Sir Isaac and Lady Wolfson, London.

The scene on this screen shows three figures climbing a narrow mountain path, between towering rocks and trees. The technique used by the jade carver is here brought into line with the conventions used by Chinese painters for depicting different kinds of foliage, rocks and clouds.

Carved on the back of this screen are bats flying among clouds. The character for bat and the character for happiness are written in different ways, but have the same pronunciation—hence the bat is used as a symbol for happiness. Happiness being considered as essential for long life, and the fact that the bat is believed to live to a great age, the symbolic meaning of the bat has been extended to include good wishes for a long life.

Plate 33 *A rhyton*. 1787. Height: 6 in. (15 cm.). China. Fitzwilliam Museum, Cambridge.

Inside the lip of this ritual vessel is an inscription pointing out the special qualities of the jade, and stating that it was sent as tribute 'by the Mohammedans'. This inscription bears the signature of the Emperor Ch'ien-lung (1736–1795) and is dated with a year corresponding to 1787.

This rhyton shape was first used during the T'ang dynasty (A.D. 618–906) in pottery. It is thought that it was first used for jade during the Sung period.

The low relief decoration is based on early bronze motives, with a series of *tao t'ieh* masks (see page 22) on the band around the top. The handle is formed by the body of a dragon whose tail curls under the bowl.

Plate 34 *Belt buckle with jade panels.* 18th century. Length: 4 in. (10 cm.). China. Mr. G. de Menasce, O.B.E., London.

This beautiful gilt copper buckle has inset panels of dark green jade, with tourmaline beads, and carved white jade ends.

Plate 35 *Vase in the shape of a lotus leaf.* Probably 19th century. Height: 12 in. (30.5 cm.). China. Fitzwilliam Museum, Cambridge.

The bowl of this vase consists of a large lotus leaf, with a lotus flower rising behind and surrounded by birds. The entwined stems of the base supporting the bowl and the elaborate carving of the upper part show the considerable technical virtuosity achieved by jade carvers in later times.

Plate 36 *Two Imperial seals.* Late 19th century. Right: 5 in. (12.5 cm.). Left: 5³/₄ in. (14.5 cm.). China. Fitzwilliam Museum, Cambridge.

The use of a seal as a mark of personal ownership dates back as far as the Shang dynasty. Jade was used for making seals at least as early as the Eastern Chou period, and in later times was usually reserved for making Imperial seals. The two examples shown in this plate are said to have belonged to the Emperor Kuang-hsü (1874–1908) and his mother the Empress Dowager, Tzu-hsi. The seals were looted during the Boxer troubles in 1900 with three other seals, one in jade and the others in soapstone. They were bought by an American journalist in Tientsin and he offered them for sale at public auction in London in 1902. The sale catalogue described them as having been the property of the Empress of China. Questions were asked in Parliament as to whether these seals were stolen property and should be returned to the Chinese government. When it was found that they were not the property of a British subject, it was decided that no action could be taken.

Both seals have entwined dragons on the top. The border of the Emperor's seal (lying flat) is decorated with dragons, and the border of the Empress's seal (shown standing on its end) with phoenixes.

Plate 37 *Jade animals.* 1930s. Height of elephant: 2½ in. (6.5 cm.). China. Mrs S. Howard Hansford.

These six small animals are examples of contemporary Chinese jade carving and were bought by Mrs Hansford from jade shops in Peking during the years 1938 and 1939. The colours of these animals, especially the deep blue of the elephant and the clear blue of the two buffaloes, are rarely encountered in jade.

The bulk of modern jade carving has been in the familiar 'jade green' jewellery mass-produced for foreign markets.

Plate 38 *Jug.* 1417–49. Height: 5³/₄ in. (14.5 cm.). Samarkand or Persia. Museu Nacional de Arte Antigua, Gulbenkian Foundation, Oeiras, Portugal.

Round the neck of this jug is an inscription in Arabic characters with the name and titles of Ulugh Beg, son of Shah Rukh and grandson of Timur. The titles include that adopted by Ulugh Beg in 1417; he died in 1449. This jug passed into the possession of the Mughal Emperor Jahangir and his son Shah Jehan. Both their names have been inscribed on the jug.

Plate 39 *Drinking vessel.* 1647. Length 6³/₄ in. (17 cm.). India, Mughal. British Museum, London.

This shallow gourd-shaped cup is inscribed with the name of Shah Jehan and a date corresponding to the year 1647.

Plate 40 *Drinking cup.* Late 17th century. Length: 8½ in. (22 cm.). Width: 5¼ in. (13.5 cm.). India, Mughal. Victoria and Albert Museum, London.

This delicate, shallow drinking cup is carved in the shape of a flower with small handles on either side representing birds' heads with the eyes inlaid in red. Flowers carved on the outer side of the cup are seen faintly on the inner side through the translucent, thin jade.

Plate 41 *Cup with an ibex head handle* (view of underside). 1657. Height: 2½ in. (6.5 cm.). Length: 7½ in. (19 cm.). Indian, Mughal. Victoria and Albert Museum, London.

This cup is carved in the shape of a gourd, one end of which becomes the head of a mountain goat. The gourd stands on a lotus blossom, from which acanthus leaves rise between the lobes of the gourd. The shape and decoration of this cup are a marvellous synthesis of the plant and animal forms that were so much favoured in Mughal times.

Engraved on one end of the cup is a small cartouche containing an inscription with the titles that Shah Jehan adopted after his accession, and a date corresponding to the year 1657.

Plate 42 *A terrapin.* Possibly 17th century. Length: 19³/₄ in. (50 cm.). India, Mughal. British Museum, London.

This terrapin of blue-green jade was discovered in the nineteenth century, buried in mud at the bottom of a reservoir in Allahabad, India. It was thought at first to be of Chinese origin but is now attributed to Mughal craftsmen. The type of terrapin represented belongs to a species called *kachuga dhongoka*, which is found only in northern India. This is an exceptionally large piece of jade carving and weighs 90 lbs.

Plate 43 *Mirror back.* Possibly 18th century. Length: 5¼ in. (13.5 cm.). Width: 4½ in. (11.5 cm.). India, Mughal. Victoria and Albert Museum, London.

This beautiful object is carved from greenish-black jade

inlaid with white jade and patterned with a formal motif in gold and rubies. The mirror itself is of glass.

Plate 44 Hukka *bowl*. 18th century. Height, with stand 20 in. Height of bowl 7³/₄ in. (19 cm.). India, Mughal. British Museum, London.

This Mughal *hukka* bowl (or *hookah*; part of a smoking pipe), is carved from a single piece of white jade inlaid with gold, spinal rubies and semi-precious stones. The bowl is one of a pair; both are mounted on identical ormulu stands of European origin. It is thought that these bowls may have belonged to the eighteenth-century eccentric William Beckford of Fonthill Abbey, Wiltshire.

Plate 45 *Three dagger handles*. Left: 18th century. Length: 5½ in. (14 cm.). Centre: possibly 17th century. Length: 5 in. (13 cm.). Right: 18th century. Length: 5 in. (13.5 cm.). India, Mughal. Victoria and Albert Museum, London.

The dagger handle on the left is carved from dark green jade inlaid in gold with a delicate tracery of foliage; the handle in the centre is carved from dark green jade, inlaid with white jade, gold and rubies and the blue-grey dagger handle on the right is carved in the shape of a horse's head and inlaid with gold and rubies. These dagger handles were worn as part of ceremonial court dress and were highly prized collectors' objects.

Plate 46 *Two hei-tikis*. Left: 6³/₄ in. (17 cm.). Right: 7 in. (17.5 cm.). New Zealand. Museum of Archaeology and Ethnology, Cambridge.

The eyes on the *hei-tiki* on the left are inlaid with *hahotis* shell, probably to represent the iris. Later examples, made after the coming of the European settlers, sometimes have red sealing wax in place of the shell. Sealing wax may also have been used to replace the shell that had fallen out of older examples. These pendants are among the most striking objects, both artistically and technically, made by the Maoris.

Plate 47 *Mere (patu pounamu)*. Length: 17 in. (43 cm.). New Zealand. Museum of Archaeology and Ethnology, Cambridge.

This is a fine example of a *mere* or ritual axe, carved from dark green nephrite. See page 33.

Plate 48 *Maori ornaments*. Left: *fish-shaped pendant*. Width: 4½ in. (11 cm.). Centre: peka peka *type of neck or ear pendant*. Width: 2¼ in. (5.5 cm.). Right: poriaka, *a leg ring for a captive parrot*. Width: 2 in. (5 cm.). Front: rapeu *drop pendant*. Length 2½ in. (6.5 cm.). New Zealand. Museum of Archaeology and Ethnology, Cambridge.

The *peka peka* in the centre, which represents the heads of two monster birds, is unfinished. It is made from a fine piece of even-coloured stone, and the carving as far as it has been done is of very high quality.

The drop pendant in the front comes from the collection of the Earl of Sandwich. It was among the objects collected by Captain Cook during his visit to New Zealand in 1869 and presented to the Earl who had provided some of the

funds necessary to finance the voyage. It is a pendant for hanging from the ear.

Plate 49 *Mask* Olmec style (800–400 B.C.). Height 8¼ in. (20.5 cm.). Mexico. Dumbarton Oaks, Washington. Robert Woods Bliss Collection.

The inside of this fearsome green jade mask is hollowed out to follow the contours of the exterior, suggesting that it was made to be worn.

Plate 50 *The Pomona flare*. Proto-Classic (about A.D. 100 –300). Diameter: 7 in. (17.5 cm.). Maya. Pomona, Belize. British Museum, London.

The surface of this flare is decorated with four sets of glyphs executed in archaic style suggesting that it may be of an early date. It was found at the Pomona fruit estate in Belize and is the most remarkable of the jades found in this area. The inscription has not yet been interpreted, but is thought to represent the four directions.

Plate 51 *Two flares*. Left: 1³/₄ in. (4.5 cm.). Right: 1³/₄ in. (4.5 cm.). Maya. Pomona, Belize. British Museum, London.

These two flares were intended to be worn in the lobes of the ear. Children had their lobes pierced at about the age of twelve, so that they could wear these ornaments. The Maize God statue in figure 8 shows this deity wearing flares of this type in its ears and over its forehead.

Plate 52 *Plaque*. Late Classic period (A.D. 600–900). Height: 5½ in. (14 cm.). Maya, said to have come from Copan, in Honduras. British Museum, London.

The design on this plaque shows a Maya dignitary sitting on a throne. He is wearing a fantastic headdress and is inclined slightly towards a small figure, possibly a prisoner or supplicant. The workmanship of this plaque represents the peak of the Maya jade carvers' skill.

Plate 53 *Mask*. Late Classic period (A.D. 600–900). Height: 7 in. (17.5 cm.). Possibly from Copan, in Honduras. British Museum, London.

A mask similar to this piece can be seen hanging round the neck of the Maize God in figure 7.

Plate 54 *Rabbit* Aztec (1367–1521). Height: 7 in. (18 cm.). Mexico. Dumbarton Oaks, Washington. Robert Woods Bliss Collection.

The eyes of this rabbit were once inlaid. It is wearing a belt that is decorated with skulls and crossbonnes at the back and in the front with the head of a warrior wearing an eagle helmet. It is said to have been found at Cempoala, state of Veracruz, Mexico.

The Rabbit was the name of a day in the Aztec calender that was connected in divination with good luck, fertility and the goddess Mayahuel. This goddess symbolised the maguey plant, grown for its spines and fibres, and for making an intoxicating drink. From its association with this goddess, the rabbit became the god of intoxication, which was a serious crime among the Aztecs. The Rabbit gods were also associated with the harvest and the moon.

3

4

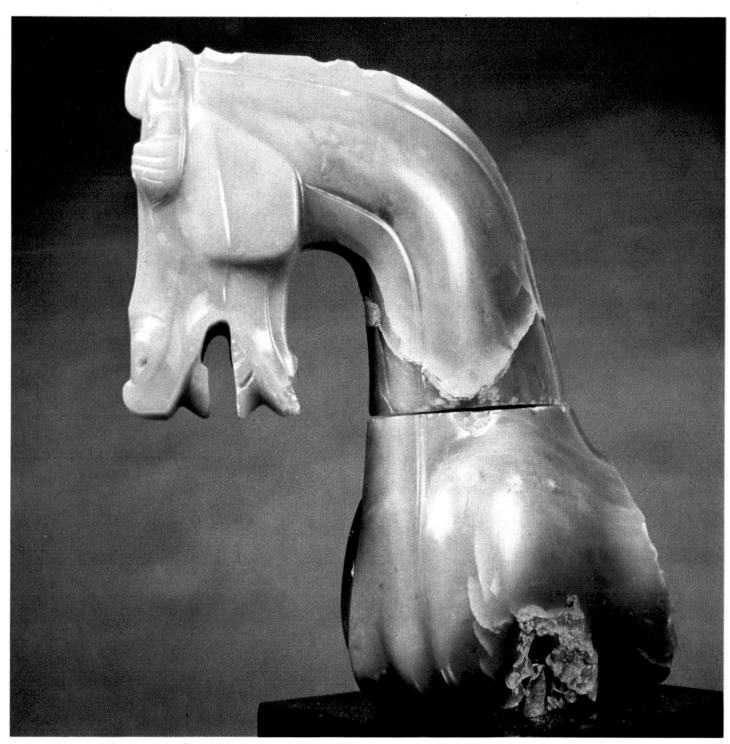

11

13

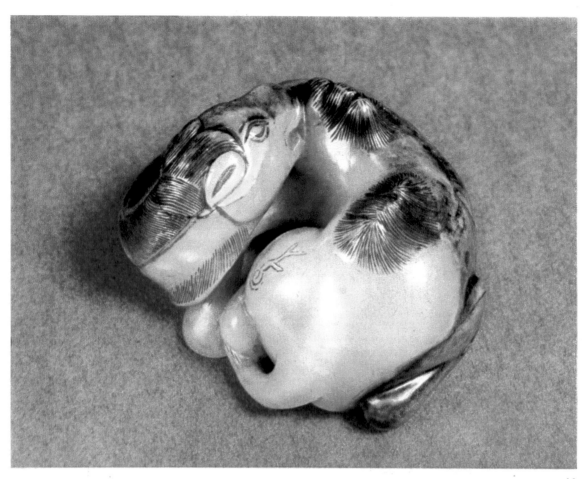

14

15

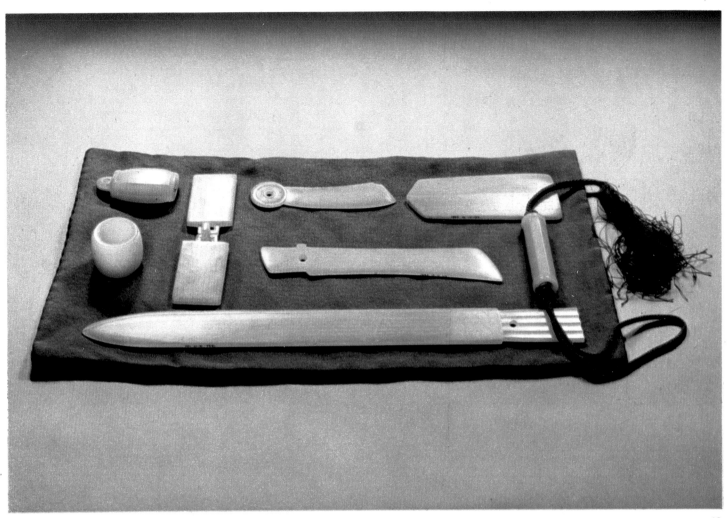

19

20

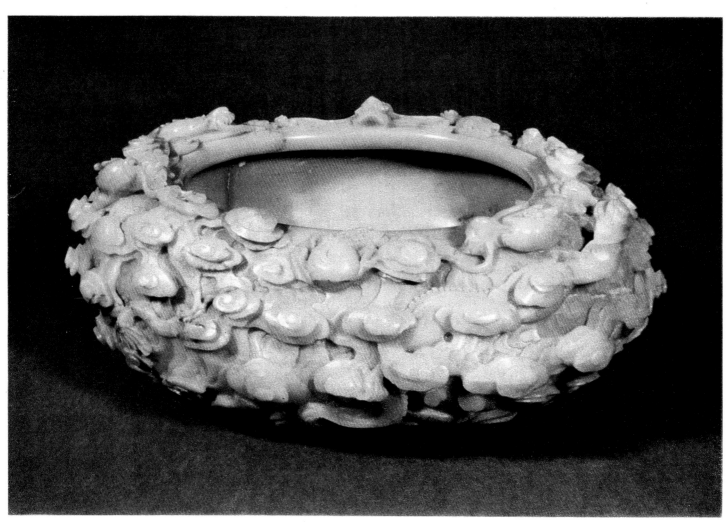

26

30

31

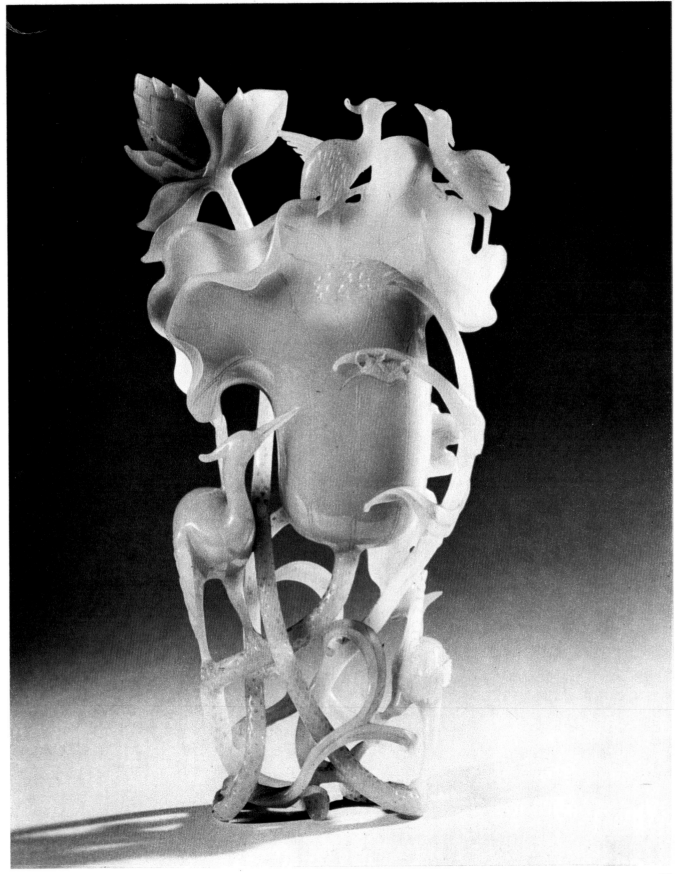

39

40

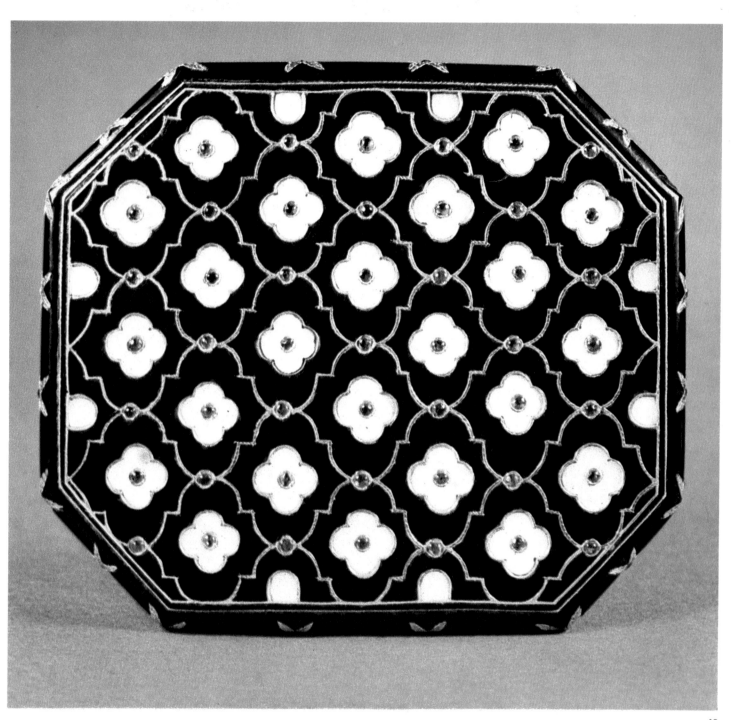

45

46

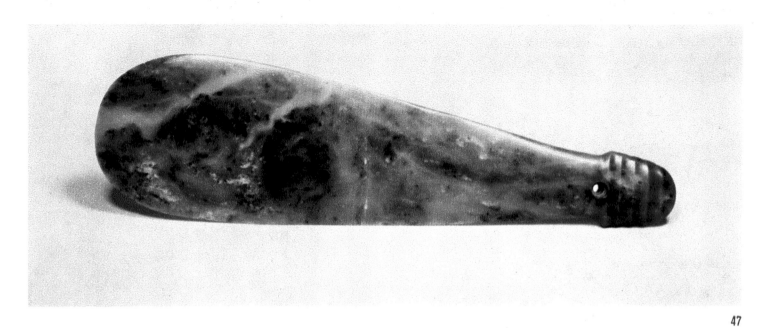

47

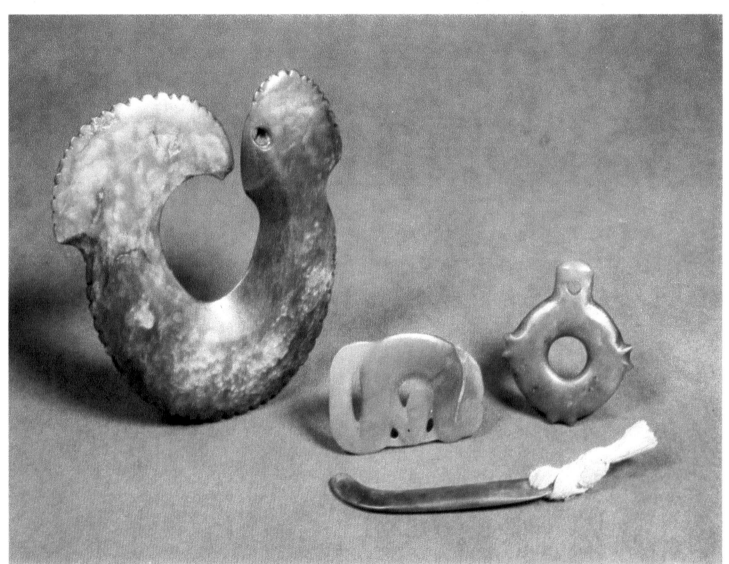

48

51